The Smart Girl's Guide to
Graduate School Success

Goal Auzeen Saedi, Ph.D.

Corby Books
Notre Dame, IN

Phdiva:

The Smart Girl's Guide to Graduate School Success

10 9 8 7 6 5 4 3 2 1

ISBN 978-0-9961362-1-1

Manufactured in the United States of America

Published by Corby Books
A Division of Corby Publishing
P.O. Box 93
Notre Dame, Indiana 46556
(574) 784-3482
www.corbypublishig.com

Contents

Part I

Priming: The College Years

MARRIAGE vs. The Ph.D.

	Marriage	Ph.D.
Typical Length:	7.5 years	7 years
Begins with:	A proposal	A thesis proposal
Culminates in a ceremony where you walk down an aisle dressed in a gown:		✔
Usually entered into by:	Foolish young people in love	Foolish young people without a job
50% end in:	Bitter divorce	Bitter remorse
Involves exchange of:	Vows	Know-how
Until death do you part?	If you're lucky	If you're lazy

CHAPTER 1

THE BASICS

"The roots of education are bitter, but the fruit is sweet."
—*Aristotle*

THE ULTIMATE COMMITMENT

Perhaps the most accurate and comical analogy to getting a Ph.D. was illustrated by the brains at Ph.D. Comics (left). They illustrate the parallels between marriage and this major academic undertaking. As such, graduate school entry is a serious decision and significant commitment. For centuries we have determined that marriage is one of the biggest decisions in women's lives. You may choose to consider what your spouse does professionally, how you relate to each other, shared interests, communication. Does one of you want three children while the other desires only one? Together you will determine where to live, how to do your financial planning, what vacation to take, and so forth as your lives become interwoven.

Rarely is the road to the Ph.D. explained to us as such. This, too, encompasses many of the facets that may make or break a marriage. In the case of graduate school, the advisor stands in for the spouse, with nearly as much clout in your future. What grants will you apply for to obtain funding? How well do the two of you communicate your needs and future plans ("I need you to run these experiments" and "I need you to look at my thesis document.")? It is not unheard of for an advisor to relocate to a new institution across the country and take their graduate students with them. Your advisor's pregnancy may in part become your pregnancy as defense dates may start to revolve around the delivery and maternity leave dates. Sabbaticals, tenure, or lack thereof may be another animal to tackle entirely.

We have seen the image in old movies where the mother's bride sheds tears on her daughter's wedding day; as her daughter drives off toward the sunset, the mother shouts to her new son-in-law, "Take good care of her!" Ironically this same mentality applies in graduate school. Why is it though that we rarely hear of such analogies? Perhaps it is because statistics show that no more than 2% of the population actually obtains a Ph.D. degree. It is considered a rarity and lofty accomplishment, bringing with it a sort of mystique that transcends little more than hushed conversations.

REALITY: graduate school is actually not that hard. While it certainly is not a barefoot walk along the beach with the water lapping softly at your ankles, it's not the tidal wave that knocks you to the ground either. Many describe the Ph.D. journey as a long and arduous road. It is fraught with disasters, anxiety, bitterness, and burnout. We often picture long nights with stained coffee mugs in front of a computer screen.

One of my undergraduate students once so aptly put it this way: "Usually when I think of grad students, I think of guys who are unshaven, have pit stains, and need a haircut." I'd say it was safe to say this student—along long with many of the others I've taught over the years—probably was often confused that I've made it this far while still looking like a regular hygienic human being. Add a sense of humor, personality, and even a little bit of kindness, and, as far as graduate students stereotypes are concerned, you're an alien form. But it need not be this way.

The truth was once put so eloquently by one of my undergraduate professors who'd received his Ph.D. at Harvard. He essentially said that once you're in, your Ph.D. is waiting for you. You have all the necessary academic knowledge and tools to succeed. The institutions would not have admitted you in the first place if they did not think you could pass the courses. The challenge is making it through.

If you are able to focus on getting from point A to point B without getting distracted, are a self-starter, and have some general direction and interest in your field, you are pretty much golden. And most people are this way when they begin this journey. But anything from departmental politics to interpersonal conflicts get in the way. I'd argue even misbehaving data (i.e., your hypotheses are not supported) will not get in the way of you completing your degree. But suddenly deciding that finding "Mr. Right" would solve all your life woes most certainly will. So will constantly comparing yourself to all of your friends who did not choose a Ph.D. who are now homeowners, complete with that coveted KitchenAid mixer.

As a card-carrying member of the Ph.D. club and therapist to many graduate students, I see the same thing time and again. Students enter academia excited about learning, research, and contributing to the field. But over time they transform and often it is not for the better. They lose the sense of confidence they had upon entering the field. They question themselves, their work, and even their sense of purpose. Fellow students put doubts in their minds. Their advisor may mistreat them, and their families may not understand what they are doing with their lives. "You know, you're in your reproductive prime right now…shouldn't you be having babies?" they ask.

I will say it many times throughout this book. There is no reason not to be able to achieve your goal of obtaining your Ph.D. upon careful and thoughtful planning. The decisions you make early on will affect you for the duration of your degree and program. Everything from location to your advisor and funding can add up to significantly alter your experience.

I'll let you in on one of my secrets. I don't know that if I was not at my particular graduate institution with my specific advisor and exact funding structure that I would have been out the door in four years time and off at my clinical internship otherwise. So if you're still in college, then you're in luck because we can start early together before any major missteps are made. And even then, we can still work out the kinks. If you're already in graduate school, congratulations, because you are already in! If you've picked up this volume at the tail end of graduate school, it is still a most excellent time to take a deep breath and fill yourself with a renewed sense of energy and hope. It can be a time to recapture the youthful spirit and love of learning that led you to where you stand today.

The road to graduate school can be a bumpy one. One might even liken it to rollercoaster ride—one minute you are at the top of the world looking out at a beautiful view, and the next you are crashing down full speed with your heart racing. There is the good and the bad all mixed in like salty and sweet kettle corn. The truth is that much of the fun in roller coasters comes from the unexpected ups and downs, but also knowing that in the end you will land back on solid ground again.

Your Turn!

★ *PhDreaming: Make a pros and cons list to entering the marital contract of graduate school. Evaluate your top reasons and motivators for graduate study. Is it the prestige factor? That someone will call you "doctor" one day? That's okay, if they are your primary motivators. Perhaps you want independence to run your own studies, mentor students, teach, contribute to the field. Write it down—what makes graduate school attractive and unattractive to you?*

NOT JUST NETWORKS, FRIENDSHIPS

One of the key elements that many strong and successful women return to time and again in identifying the keys to their successes across the lifespan involves their friendships. When upset, frustrated, or even jumping for joy, a first response often involves sharing this news with others whether it is through a phone call, text message, or email. As such, it doesn't need much saying that our numerous relationships and friendships contribute significantly to our support networks and well-being.

In today's world we have been taught that it's all about the networking. You may be "addicted" in the colloquial way to Facebook, Twitter, Instagram, and any other forms of social media. You may use tools such as LinkedIn to professionally expand your networks further. But to the shy and quiet girl who prefers working alone in lab, or who likes to come out of her shell on rare occasions, the word "networking" sounds just pain awful. In reality, although important, networks aren't everything. They may help you skip a few steps on your way up the ladder, but it is the friends who will grab your hand and pull you up should you slip or loose your footing along the way.

During my undergraduate years I recall feeling that graduate school applications required the greatest secrecy and solitude. I didn't wish to share my essays, or even just my woes. This was a great mistake. It wasn't until graduate school when I was truly alone for the first time that I came to realize how important it was to maintain and sustain friendships. I can't recall what it was at the time that prompted it, but I do remember picking up the phone one day and calling an old friend. We'd just graduated from college together and had worked together in a student group. I'd been, shall we say, a challenging president to work with, and she had put up with all of that, so that alone told me how amazing she was. Though the details are fuzzy now, I recall what a great comfort she'd provided during my early transition into graduate school. We had both moved to smaller, more remote towns in an attempt to receive doctorate degrees without so much as a clue as to how we were going to do it. We were panicked and we were afraid. But we had each other. And pretty soon every Saturday we had a standing phone date. We'd share our hopes, but also our fears. Our doubts and our uncertainties about the decisions we'd made. We were adjusting and at times a mess. But neither of us had to go it alone.

The friendship taught me more than I could imagine. I learned about myself in so many ways. In other words, I was vulnerable and I owned it. I didn't need to pretend I had unwavering confidence or that things were okay when they were not. It also taught me that those of us who seem the most "together" rarely are. I learned of the importance of reaching out, giving, and receiving. Though the phone dates dried up over the years, in that first year they were truly crucial to my survival. In time, I made many friends as did she with fellow graduate students and we built our own new communities.

Through internships, fellowships, and new jobs, graduate school may require adjustment after adjustment for nearly a decade's worth of time. Wherever one may be in the journey, reaching out and connecting with others may be one of the most critical things you do for your survival. In my time as a college mental health therapist, I'd often see that the most distressed and hopeless students I'd treated had also been the ones who were most alone and isolated. Think about this as you decide where to live and what program feels like it has a good vibe. For some the hustle and bustle of a big city can provide countless social opportunities, while for others it can feel more alienating. For each of us connectedness can look different and understanding one's own style can be important.

As such, I encourage you, the reader, to take these factors into consideration. Think about your friendships, those you have and those you wish to deepen. Whether you may take action by creating an applicant support group of sorts that meets monthly or you find a buddy to pair off with, do not go it alone. It is not necessary and may only make you feel more stressed and isolated. You can connect in person, or even through Skype or FaceTime. At the very least, remember the old adage about misery loving company! In fact, social psychology research has supported this very notion, so surround yourself with compassionate others in bumpy times.

Your Turn!

★ *PhDialing: Pick up that phone wherever you may be in the process and reach out. Commit to making even one short phone call to a friend, family member, mentor, or loved one over the next week. Trust me on this one, just do it!*

IF ELLE WOODS CAN BE A LAWYER THEN....

When you think of scholarly role models, the name Elle Woods rarely comes to mind. A fictional character with Barbie-doll looks clad in hot pink, heels, and trailed by a Chihuahua hardly seems to fit the image of one with high academic prowess. And yet, for one generation of aspiring career-bound women, she has been what some may consider an inspiration. Certainly for me, she was what landed me in a top 20 school. Her tenacity paired with her exuberant and optimistic attitude was not just comical, but admirable. It is for this reason that I ask us to take pause for a moment and consider the case of Elle.

In the film *Legally Blonde*, Elle Woods typifies the academic outcast. For in the movie, extremes of the feminist spectrum are displayed. There is her mean and catty trophy husband-seeking rival on one side, and a liberal bra-burning lesbian who wants to change the name "semester" to "ovester" on the other. She fits nowhere in between, nor does she boast the scholastic achievements of her Harvard classmates she learns during orientation.

In essence, Elle lands herself at Harvard Law through an ostentatious video essay in an attempt to win back her boyfriend (dramatic liberties taken by script writers with respect to reality, we know). And yet, despite a strong GPA, LSAT scores, and record of leadership and community service, she is discounted completely. She is ridiculed and excluded time and again. She is not allowed to join a study group, as the members deem it "a smart people thing" that precludes her from joining. And in the final straw, when her ex-boyfriend suggests to her she is not smart enough to complete law school and win a prestigious internship, she asks, "Did we not just get into the same law school?" Eventually fed up and alone, with her only friend being a manicurist, she proclaims, "I'll show you how valuable Elle Woods can be." And herein lies my purpose in considering her case.

In my initial quest to gain admissions into graduate school, I was told time and again how incredibly competitive a Ph.D. in clinical psychology was. The first three people I spoke to who were either in graduate programs or professors in psychology all told me to pick another career. Social work is a shorter program. Industrial organizational psychology is where the money is. Most people get rejected from clinical programs, be ready to re-apply next year. These were the messages I received.

Not to be deterred, six years ago, I recalled the spirit of Elle. Albeit sounding downright bizarre, I thought to myself, why can't one smile and take all the negativity in stride like her? If graduate school entry can often be a pretty strategic and straightforward path (grades, scores, letters, essays, research, publications, etc.), then should it really matter if the person filling out the application wears thick glasses or glitter eye shadow? Who is to flippantly say I'm not qualified?

So in a huge leap of faith, I threw out the rubric. I did not apply to the 20 graduate programs every graduate school guide recommended. I chose five instead. I landed my top choice,

Notre Dame, as well as an Ivy League school. How? Certainly five years of hard work and many strategies I'll be sharing in the first part of this book. But above all was a belief that who was to say that I couldn't make a dream come true? So whether it is Elle Woods, Princess Diana, Barbara Walters, Oprah, or Michelle Obama, remember the powerful women who made it when few would have ever predicted their incredible and awe-inspiring contributions. Then remember why you are choosing to embark on this amazing journey of graduate school. And yes, if you are still with me after I just posited Elle Woods as an academic role model without so much as an eye roll, then we are exactly where we need to be.

Your Turn!

★ *PhDiscovery: Pick out a mentor or role model whose journey inspires you. It can be an author, political figure, activist, advocate, friend, or family member. Think about what makes them so inspirational and what elements you'd like to absorb. Perhaps it is humor, spirit, or artistic talent. See if you can't start to cultivate these seeds in yourself.*

A NEW WAVE OF FEMINISM: THE RISE OF THE PHDIVA

Throughout this book, I will be taking what many may deem an "unconventional" approach to viewing and discussing academia. My fellow feminist scholars may take one look at the title of this book and think, "PhDiva!? We must have just gone backwards 50 years in the feminist movement"—which is precisely why this book is titled and presented as it is.

Historically throughout the academy there has been an implicit message to women that in order to become successful, we must essentially hide our femininity and aspire to masculine ideals. Traditionally "feminine" and "masculine" traits are ones that I'd argue both men and women ought to embody. Who doesn't appreciate a man who is a sensitive and caring listener, or a woman who can change her own flat tire? However, the traits most often associated with professional success have traditionally been male-oriented. What happens, though, if we see things in another light? What if we played devil's advocate and list the traditional "female" traits? They might include things like relational ability, communication, negotiation, and mediation. Wouldn't these traits be equally if not more in demand for professional success in any number of top positions? Let's time travel back a century and praise women for their artistic achievements, such as home décor. Wouldn't offices be more aesthetically pleasing and lead to greater productivity? Wouldn't customers be more likely to shop in these stores and return? In truth, it is all about the perspective that we choose to take.

Too often though for being a highly educated group, scholars suffer from their own cognitive rigidities. Many of academia's history and legacies continue for generations often times more out of tradition than true rhyme or reason. One of the byproducts of this system is that women's progress has often been stagnant.

According to statistics, women hold more non-tenure track positions than men and hold fewer percentages of tenure. In 2006, men held 77% of president positions in colleges. Women make up 45% of senior administrators and 38% of chief academic officers, and earn less than male faculty members across all ranks and institution types. Even in psychology, a field that many associate as a "soft science" covering "touchy feely" topics (not actually true), men still rule the playing field.

It is unsurprising then that women in clinical and counseling programs, for example, are more likely to pursue applied work in areas such as therapy than enter the competition for tenure-track faculty positions. Counseling settings are often less ruthless and likely to promote egalitarian values. Having been on the receiving end of journal feedback, ranging from respectful and supportive to condescending and rude, I can certainly empathize.

But what about another type of academic, and another brand of feminism? Enter what I propose to be the PhDiva. My guess would be that many would have one of three reactions: cringing, rejoicing, or shaking their heads in confusion. That said, I ask, why not? Women are often judged against and in comparison to men—not as an independent entity. Whatever men do, we think about how we measure up, and often are unsatisfied with the result. But it does not have to be about who does it better. What about the notion that women make up their own rules, play by them, and conquer whatever field they choose?

I am often in awe of the lengths that women go to in academia to hide their femininity. I recall conversations with graduate women who would tell me about books they'd read that told them how to dress and present themselves to be taken seriously. Naturally I don't recall the details, likely because somewhere after "skirt below the knees" I started to feel insulted. I even remember colleagues who would take off their nail polish before meetings with advisors to appear more professional. But the real question is, so what if you like to wear Tiffany blue nail polish and a tiny bit of a heel while frantically typing away at your manuscript? Since when did a woman's own decision to look nice for herself become problematic? After all, we are not promoting inappropriateness and self-objectification, but rather a sense of pride and well, heaven forbid, style. Certainly, I'm not advising that women start going into lab with miniskirts, stilettos, and low-cut skintight leopard-print tops. But I am suggesting that women be comfortable in their own skin, whatever that may look like for them.

We have often seen how the media treats prominent political figures when they are women. Did we ever care what suits the Bushes or Clinton wore? No, but we do know where Michelle Obama got that dress and what color palette Hilary Clinton chose when running for president. All of a sudden the spotlight is less about these women's credentials and more about where they shop and how their latest haircut looks. Unfortunately for women, the choice has been crudely put about being oriented toward looks or books.

This leads me to the observation that women have once again been on the losing side with respect to professional achievement. As a statistical minority in graduate programs across the country, they struggle to fit themselves into a mold that was never made for them. They become anxious, many times depressed. They must hide their inner selves for fear of judgment or rejection. But I ask, why can't we be true to ourselves? Some women wish to go to lab meetings with their comfortable yoga pants on, while others like some sparkles. Let's just deal with it. It doesn't decrease their IQ, ability, or competence in the least. So I ask, PhDiva? Don't mind if we do.

Your Turn!

★ *PhDeserving: Stop for a moment and just recognize your accomplishments to date as a woman. Note that you deserve this recognition. Reflect upon what it means to be a woman as well as all the other identities you may hold. They may include race, spirituality, sexual orientation, ethnicity, ability status, socioeconomic status, age, and various areas of privilege or minority status. Think about how all of these aspects of your identity shape you and what it means to truly be yourself without worry of being judged. Make a commitment early on to stay true to yourself. Later you will come to adopt aspects of a professional identity. But that should not be counter to or contradict the values you hold closest to you. Write a letter to yourself about who you are and for what you stand. Look back at this every so often throughout the process in times of doubt and uncertainty.*

CHAPTER 2

THE ESSENTIALS

"Nothing is to be feared, only understood."

—*Dr. Marie Curie*

DOUBLE MAJOR OR DOUBLE MOCHA?

"Is graduate study for you?" "Should you get a Master's degree before applying?" "Who should you ask to be a recommender?" It was not too long ago that I was posed such questions as I pored over countless graduate school preparation books and materials. I contemplated whether or not the "tiered" approach of applying to safety and wish-list schools made any sense, considering my energy would be split among 20 school applications rather than the five or so I had in mind. I also thought about how much contact with my future advisor would be appropriate, attempting to achieve the balance between seeming professionally interested and obsessively desperate. Ultimately, I followed some of the advice I read and did the exact opposite of other tips. In this chapter, I will chronicle factors for consideration in preparation for graduate school.

At the simplest level, we begin with the academic major and overall well-rounded nature of an educational program. Early on in my process, I spent far too much time worrying that I came from a large state school that no one had ever heard of. And yet, I went on to train at Notre Dame, Berkeley, and Stanford. It's true what they say about not "psyching" yourself out. While a certain degree of anxiety is completely natural and good for you, letting it overwhelm and take over can do more harm than anything else. Instead of spending time worried that you're not at Princeton, think critically about how you can maximize where you are. Large schools offer a huge variety of courses never to be found in small liberal arts colleges. On the other hand, the smaller private schools can allow for more one-on-one attention and letters of recommendation from individuals who can truly say they knew you for four years (more on letter writers later). The overarching point is look at your environment and own it. Further, make it about you.

Many graduate school "gurus," so to speak, suggest lengthy lists of courses to take prior to graduate school that look daunting at best. They may want extra statistics courses, a class in computer science, and who knows what else. While it is important to take courses that will later relate to your graduate program, don't allow yourself to fall into the maximize, maximize, maximize plan either. It is very important to strike a balance between being an impressive candidate with breadth and depth of training, while taking care of your sanity.

Start out as early as you can by creating a rough sketch of what you'd like your undergraduate career to look like. Below I'll sketch a sample draft based off of my field in psychology (and in actuality many of the courses I took). Know that you will have dozens of iterations of this roadmap, but that you can keep making adjustments without any unpleasant surprises (e.g., realizing at the last minute you must take a general educational requirement that conflicts with the one course you've been looking forward to for the last year or so). You can fill out a draft schedule in Appendix A.

DRAFTING OUT YOUR GAME PLAN
Freshman Year

Fall	Winter	Spring
Intro Stats -4 units	Intro Stats II-4 units	Research Methods-4 units
General Ed Course-4 units	General Ed Course-4 units	Psych of Women- 4 units
General Ed Section-1 unit	General Ed Section-1 unit	General Ed Course- 4 units
Intro Psych-4 units	Intro Psych II-4 units	General Ed Section-1 unit
Volunteer research assistant	Volunteer research assistant	Volunteer research assistant
		PE: Gentle Yoga Fitness-1 unit

Sophomore Year

Fall	Winter	Spring
Intro Biology-3 units	Social Psychology I- 4 units	Language Requirement-4 units
Biology Lab-1 unit	Motivation- 4 units	Behavior Analysis-4 units
Language Requirement-4 units	Language Requirement-4 units	Behavioral Neuroscience-4 units
Human Development-4 units	Volunteer research assistant	Meds & Psychopathology-4 units
Paid Research Assistant	*tested out of 1 quarter of language to save time	Research Credits: Mental Health & Military-2 units
	Paid Research Assistant	PE: Dance Class- 1 unit
		Paid Research Assistant

Junior Year

Fall	Winter	Spring
Experimental Psych-4 units	History & Systems Psych-4 units	Social Psych II-4 units
Health Psych-4 units	Emotions in the Brain-4 units	Personality-4 units
Research Credits: Clinical Neuropsych-3 units	Physiological Psych-4 units	Prac: Peer Advising-2 units
Research Credits: Attributional	Research Credits: Ethnicity & Perfectionism-2 units	Research Credits: Ethnicity & Perfectionism-2 units
Processes-2 units	Research Credits: Attributional Processes-2 units	Paid Research Assistant
PE: Dance Class-1 unit		
Paid Research Assistant	Paid Research Assistant	

Senior Year

Fall	Winter	Spring
Film Genres in Context-4 units	Film History-4 units	Meditation Capstone- 6 units
Special Studies: Leadership-2 units (Honor Society President)	Special Studies: Leadership-2 units (Honor Society President)	Special Studies: Leadership-2 units (Honor Society President)
Prac: Peer Advising-2 units	Research Credits: Ethnicity & Perfectionism-2 units	Prac: Public Health-3 units (for paid research assisting)
Prac: Public Health-3 units (for paid research assisting)	Stardom Film Course-4 units	PE: Dance Class-1 unit
PE: Dance Class-1 unit		

A few important points you will notice from the draft schedule pertain to credits, courses, extra-curriculars, and fitness. Many students that I work with in therapy come to me stressed and over-worked. They over-estimate their abilities and wind up with severe anxiety. For financial reasons many students are forced to take the maximum amount of credits. However, even this can be made more manageable.

There are many ways I've seen students put themselves into an academic bind. Often it relates to a strict adherence or rigidity to a program that simply isn't working for them. Sometimes students will insist on that double major or two minors. The reality is that graduate admissions committees are unlikely to really care that much about the second major—other factors such as strong grades in important classes and research publications can more than make up for that. Students also regularly forget that many extra-curriculars (e.g., student groups, research labs) can take up as much time as a full-time class. If it is possible to take some of these activities for credit, it can showcase nicely on your transcript while eating up credits to save you from a fuller course load that would include midterms, finals, and other assignments.

Finally, it is important to play around with different schedule types to allow yourself breathing space and actual study time. Many of the Stanford students I worked with had every hour of every day scheduled. This left very little room for a back-up plan of any sort. What if they came down with the flu, or worse, mono? Students normally schedule their semesters and quarters assuming they are functioning at 100% capacity at all times. This is simply unrealistic. Why? Because life happens. A loved one falls ill, a parent who was financing your education loses their job, you find out that you are expecting. Any number of variables can occur. On the simplest level, many students hold part-time employment. If each hour of the day is scheduled, then where is there time to actually study for the classes one is taking or to write that paper? This is where students start to cut out time from sleep or seeing friends. Then they may start a cycle in which they start to feel over-worked, disconnected, and burnt-out. If you can take classes Monday-Thursday and take Friday "off," then consider having this full day of unscheduled time to catch up on your work. Give yourself a break—this doctor ordered it!

Your Turn!

★ *PhDrafting: Go ahead, use the draft schedule above to create a rough sketch of the next few quarters or years depending upon where you are at. Be sure it looks realistic with some enjoyable classes thrown in for good measure. Make sure you have something to look forward to. No one wants to look at a schedule on the first day of classes and dread what is to come.*

PUBLISH, PRESENT, REPEAT

There are many ways to augment (and make more manageable) your course load by finding real-world practical educations experiences. Volunteering in labs or working in the writing center for example can be means of achieving this. Word of mouth and some digging can unearth many great finds. When I was a graduate student, I had lots of data in need of transcription. There were also lots of undergraduates looking for research experience.

In my case, I also offered publication credit in the form of poster presentations as well as mentorship on obtaining undergraduate grants. In the end, it was a win-win situation. I had an enormous amount of help with my data, while my undergraduates walked away with course credit, one to two poster presentation credits on their vita, and an undergraduate research grant to boot. Not too bad!

Important in this equation is to find research mentors who will provide this. During my undergraduate years I probably worked in roughly a half-dozen labs in total. I learned to quickly terminate projects where it was clear that I was being used for the grunt work with little to no credit. As women we can be afraid of asserting ourselves and asking for things like publication credit, but it is all a matter of how we ask and being educated in what we are asking for.

For example, being put on a poster requires less effort than being an author on a research manuscript. There are also differences in how faculty approach authorship credit. To be frank, some are more generous, whereas others are downright stingy. Learning this quickly and where you stand can save you much time later on. It is a shame to be working on a research project for multiple years where undergraduate student A walks away with a publication and grant, whereas undergraduate B walks away with little more than a letter of recommendation. The bottom line, is don't be afraid to ask for what you want, but also be prepared to work for it.

Relatedly, look for the various opportunities available to help you stand out. But also make sure these are things you enjoy. For example, I worked with a professor known for having dozens of undergraduates serve as T.A.s and assist with neuropsychological assessment batteries. I came to find that I enjoyed the T.A.ship work more than the research and so devoted extra time there. As a result of taking multiple classes with this professor and working with him, I was also able to have him serve as a letter of recommendation writer. In large schools especially, it is important to keep an eye out for faculty who can get to know you on a more personal level to write strong letters. There are few times I would ever use the word "never," but I will say it this time. Never ask a professor who does not know you to serve as a letter writer. When I was training at Berkeley, I would speak with students pondering whether or not to ask the professor of a large lecture course to write them a letter. They would assume because the letter was coming from a "big name" in the field that it would automatically hold more clout. However, without a personal (and strong!) relationship with such a professor, it is highly unlikely that a letter grade is sufficient information off of which to base a recommendation. As one who has served on admissions committees, after reading dozens of letters of recommendation, it starts to become clear which are the subpar, strong, and superstar letters. The superstar letters may sometimes come from someone with a little bit less of a prestigious title, but is the one that is a glowing review of your amazing talents. Showcase this, not the generic letter from the president of a national physics society just because s/he was your professor for an introductory-level course.

Another factor that I will stress throughout this book is the importance of self-care. Notice that in my draft of courses at the end (senior year) you will see more regularity of fitness classes. Truth be told, they factored into my own schedule too late in the game. Often it can feel that getting ready for graduate school means that everything else must fall to the wayside. Life can become too extreme on any continuum. For example, I've worked with students who have a "work hard, play hard" mentality. This has translated to binge drinking, unsafe sexual behavior, drug usage, and other harmful behaviors. The idea is that they are working so hard in the middle of the week that they must reward themselves, or otherwise numb away their pain in this manner.

Integrating a healthy lifestyle throughout the process of graduate school application is essential.

Your Turn!

★ *PhDepth: Consider starting a draft curriculum vitae if you don't already have one. There are many excellent sample vita resources out there and your campus career resource center could be a great place to start. Look at not only ways of listing things and readability, but also get a sense of the typical vita headings that could use some filling out. For example, you might have lots of listings under the "academic honors and awards" section, but nothing listed where some might have "grants and scholarships." Also, decide what is most relevant. For example, at this stage "volunteer experience" can be nice for some fields, but completely irrelevant for others. Think about breadth but also depth. Then consider how you can go about filling in those missing gaps.*

GO AHEAD, BE A DIVA ABOUT IT

Throughout the graduate school application process, there are countless factors to take into consideration. Some of the factors less explored involve being true to yourself throughout the process. As I've said before, while meeting prerequisites and taking fancy courses are important, there are also ways of getting your own needs met. It's your education after all.

While earlier I discussed course planning, a key trick that can greatly enhance your chances of graduate school entry is beginning a preliminary search of schools you are interested in, and downloading the vitas of their current graduate students. Now I know this sounds like it is entering stalker territory, but I assure you it's not. Some of the best summer programs I attended were found through these vitas. You see, by examining what types of publications, internships, and so forth these students did in their undergraduate years, you can get a sense of the type of applicant a graduate program may be looking for. I found out that many students attended summer institutes through our national organization, the American Psychological Association. I even managed to get scholarships to offset the cost of attending these workshops and summer intensives. As a result, I met peers across the country (some of whom I'm still in touch with today) and had the opportunity to visit campuses ranging from Vanderbilt to Princeton and George Washington. I got a sense of the schools, the geography, and even if I'd want to go to graduate school at those places later on.

Furthermore, joining national organizations in your field is a huge asset. You can often join as a student affiliate or member for a fraction of the cost. As an added bonus, you can add it onto your vita and showcase your interest and commitment to the field as a young scholar. You learn the ins and outs and all the recent trends in the field and research. In fact, you might be just on the same page as some of the faculty you will later go on to interview with by keeping up with some of the literature in this way. Again this doesn't mean go overboard and read every journal or feel obliged to join every organizational body's membership. Just make sure to have it on your radar and know that they can offer great scholarships and grant opportunities as well.

Another benefit to organizations and summer intensives is that they can also allow you to foster and develop your own interests in a novel fashion. As someone interested in feminism and women's achievement, I found myself a summer leadership program for women with a political science bent to it. Granted, I'd never taken a political science course and didn't know quite where I'd fit it into my schedule. But through a fun one-week program I was able to visit our state capitol, make up legislative bills, and actually got to see the interaction between my own field of interest and policy. While only a week long, this experience continues to shape how I view the advancement of women, and I continue to be in touch with the women I met through this program.

Also, remember to have fun with it. An easy trap to fall into is to focus on all the benchmarks. A notorious pesky little thing is that test, you might have heard of it—the Graduate Record Exam (GRE). While you certainly cannot walk out with an exceedingly low score, it can help to know that GREs surprisingly aren't everything. In my case, I scored over the average, but really just a teeny tiny iota above it. High GPAs, grades in advanced math courses, and other criteria can make up for a lower GRE score. There are those schools that compute indices using your GRE scores and GPA as a cutoff to even look at your application. But also think to yourself—do you want to be attending an institution that places so much emphasis on numbers rather than on other personal qualities that cannot be quantitatively measured? I was impressed when, during my graduate school interview, one of the program directors remarked on my strong grades in statistics and Calculus. The Calculus was actually a class credit that had transferred from high school and the reason I had so much stats was because I was on a quarter system. That said, the fact that the director could compliment me rather than deride, as some interview horror stories have gone, told me a lot about the values and spirit of what later became my graduate program.

Finally, don't be afraid to think outside the box, or as one of my favorite sayings goes, like there is no box at all. The bulk of intense academic work prior to graduate school will often occur over the span of roughly two years—the last half of sophomore year, all of junior year, and the first half of senior year. That is, if you plan to apply for graduate school during your senior year. This leaves a full half year or so to truly enjoy yourself, and more if you plan accordingly. Once all of my major courses were done, my research manuscripts were in, I gave myself some time to enjoy another one of my interests completely unrelated to my field—film. In some ways I regret that I waited so long, as these were some of the most interesting courses I took. This was a hazard of graduate school tunnel vision. But I was able to take film history and other inspiring courses that gave me a brand new appreciation for the theatrical arts. I met professors who truly brought the medium to life and taught me to see beyond the plot to deeper themes, cultural significance, and allegory. I took the classes for no letter grade either, and so fully immersed myself in the material. It also went on to later influence my work in psychology, as I joined our media psychology division and during graduate school started my own column, combining my interests in media, film, writing, and mental health. It goes to show that sometimes stepping off the beaten path is what really allows new doors to open.

Further, thinking like there is no box at all also allows you to see your vision of your future with heightened purpose and clarity. One of the most disheartening statistics I encountered early on in my graduate school experience was around how small the likelihood was of gaining admission into a program. Being admitted into Ivy League programs and other well-respected institutions was even harder. The odds for many of the programs that interested me ranged from 1 to 7% admission rates. The message given through countless advisors and graduate school guidebooks was that applying to over a dozen schools would greatly enhance your odds of admittance. And yet, there weren't a dozen programs that interested me! Knowing exactly where I wished to go, and not having the patience to fake interest in school #15 of 20, I stuck with five schools where I felt I could be happiest and most fulfilled. Yes, I panicked over a spelling mistake on one Ivy League application (I actually managed a mistake in the punctuation of the college to which I was applying); but I was still admitted to the school, providing some assurance that all is not lost on small mistakes, however hard we strive to avoid them.

The lesson to be learned is to ignore the naysayers. They will always exist. While I am not advocating blind optimism, remember that hard work can get you very far. Thus, if you've always dreamed of attending a school, don't for a minute think they are out of your league if you have done all that you possibly could to be the best applicant possible. There are no "dream" schools.

Finally, when drowning in stacks of applications, it always helps to stand back and ask yourself why you are doing this. Are you looking towards a graduate degree because it looks impressive? Or are you embarking upon this journey because is it your calling and what you are drawn to in life? Faculty, general advisors, and, yes, counseling center therapists, may also be a fantastic source for just sharing your thoughts and anxieties. The process takes much patience and can make students vulnerable as they are deciding their fate for the next four to five plus years. I will never forget the words of our national scholarship advisor at my undergraduate institution who shared with me her observation that I was resilient. Whatever the outcome, I had the full resources to handle it she told me. And wherever I ended up, no matter what the name of the school, the quality of my work would remain constant. Just having someone tell me that was an incredible gift. In turn, I say to you, the reader, that in seeking out a book such as this and staying authentic and open-minded, you have all that it takes to succeed. Where there is heart, there is incredible strength and tenacity.

Your Turn!

★ *PhDancing: That's right, dance to the beat of your own drum. After all, that's what all of this PhDiva fuss is all about! It's about respecting some traditions but also re-writing others. It was American historian, women's history scholar, and Harvard professor Dr. Laurel Thatcher Ulrich whose runaway famous line said, "Well-behaved women seldom make history."*

CHAPTER 3

THE MUST-HAVES

"It is better to look ahead and prepare than to look back and regret."
—*Jackie Joyner-Kersee*

YOU DON'T HAVE TO STUDY FINANCE TO BE FINANCIALLY SAVVY

Perhaps I'm starting this chapter with a discussion on finances because after two years in the San Francisco bay area, I found a new appreciation for smart financial planning. Granted, these two years were my clinical internship and fellowship years so the damage was limited. However, many in California take out loans on top of other student loans to cover them while in this pricey state. In my four years in the Midwest, however, financial woes were far in the background and I was fortunate to have zero student loans. As such, here are some factors for consideration when selecting and applying to graduate programs.

One of the beauties of pursuing a Ph.D. is that typically you will be fully-funded. This is in part what makes these programs so highly competitive. When a program admits a small handful a year (if that) they are often fully funding each and every one of them. Funding structures may vary and it is important to be mindful of all the caveats. First off, I would advise starting with programs that provide full funding for the duration of the program, making sure that students actually graduate within that timeframe. For example, in my program the average time to degree completion was around five years or so, and funding lasted a full five years. This could put students in a sixth or seventh year in a bind, as funding may not be available. That said, one should not be in any program that keeps students that long anyway as an average time to degree. I once visited an Ivy League Ph.D. program for an interview and spoke with an eighth year student… in Manhattan. On top of having to find a way of funding herself, she was also doing it in one of the nation's most expensive zip codes.

Prioritizing the importance of solid funding cannot be emphasized enough. I worked with a Ph.D. student at Berkeley who was in her seventh year whose funding had stopped somewhere around year three or four when she had gotten her master's degree. There was a lot wrong with this picture, including a four-year master's degree and the fact that by the time I was working with her, she was volunteering to work in the lab she used to be paid to be a member of.

Several factors to think about with respect to funding: First, where is the money coming from? Is it a grant, departmental, or a combination of the two? Many graduate school guides make recommendations that one apply for and receive a prestigious national grant such as through the National Science Foundation. While extremely impressive, I have not yet met a graduate student who actually funded themselves this way. And I have met a lot of graduate students over the years. Just something to keep in mind. Second, how long might the grant that is funding you last? If you come onto a five-year grant in year four of five, how will the rest of your education be funded? Also, will you be tied to only that advisor and that lab? In my case, I was funded by the department which was a huge asset. For my fellow graduate students who ended up changing their interests and labs, they did not have to worry about their funding stream disappearing. Others whose funding was tied into a grant often times struggled more if the need arose to change advisors.

When funded by the department (or regardless in some cases), there is an expectation that graduate students will have an R.A.ship or T.A.ship. This basically means you will be providing service predominantly in a research capacity or teaching assistantship. By the end of graduate school it will be impossible to not have done both, but some programs may start you off with one or the other, or a combination. The duties can vary vastly as a function of the university, lab, and advisor. For example, I knew individuals whose research assistantship duties were not unlike a 9 to 5 job. They essentially clocked in and out of lab and were required to be there for a minimum number of hours on top of a full course load and their own developing research. I've also known T.A.ships to range from being the class T.A. and grading papers to single-handedly teaching multiple sections of large introductory lecture classes. The compensation is usually worded as "tuition remission" and "a living stipend." The living stipend again varies by university, region, and discipline. Engineers and the hard sciences typically make more, with humanities and social sciences being paid less. Although for many women asking about money can feel uncomfortable, it can be helpful to ask current graduate students what typical stipends looks like.

Also, some departments may provide professional development conference funding, which can be helpful. In my graduate program, all graduate students had a set amount of conference money available each year and were eligible to apply for additional grants through graduate student unions and other organizations. Typically, I was able to attend several conferences a year without much of a financial burden. However, I often met graduate students from other programs who were on their own dime. I later learned this was the actual norm; this can sometimes be the advantage of well-funded institutions.

Finally, it is very important to think about summer funding as well as competition for funding. When many graduate programs are recruiting students they may use financial promises to gain your interest. Be sure to find out exactly how the funding structure is set up. For example, it wasn't until my first year of graduate school that I learned summer funding money came from a different pot and was allotted separately than the funding we received the other nine months a year. My colleagues who were on grants already had their funds divided over 12 months and didn't worry about summer finances. For those of us unaware of this, we had a slight moment of panic to realize we would not obtain the exact same funding over the summer. We all wound up getting funded, but over the years our department came up with more stringent criteria to make sure students were justifying their need for funding (e.g., I'll be doing data collection, applying for a conference, writing a manuscript). Summer can sometimes be slacking time for students, so I got the sense the department was perhaps trying to incentivize better summer planning. However, talks later turned to whether or not summer funding should be competitive so that not all students were guaranteed funding.

Competitive funding raises a whole other set of potential concerns. I was fortunate in that, overall, the atmosphere in my department was rather collegial. No one was really competing for the same resources in a cutthroat way as there was largely enough to go around for everyone. In other departments, the picture was not always so pretty. Student evaluations, achievement benchmarks, and other factors could be used to determine who would receive what type of funding, if any. As such, be sure to land yourself in a space where the funding structure feels comfortable. One does not fully appreciate what financial stress is like until they have experienced it. At the risk of sounding like Suze Orman, I have to say it—don't underestimate the importance of ensuring strong financial security. Below is a budgeting guide that can help you get a sense of expenses to consider. When you track your money, you have a much better sense of where it's going and even if you can save a little bit for a small treat for yourself later on!

Expense Category	Cost	Considerations
Rent	$600-$2000k+	Is it on or off-campus, what is included (i.e., utilities, cable)? Is a roommate worth your financial sanity or a bigger hassle? What is the cost of living like?
Utilities	$60	Water, gas, or electric, sewage, garbage, what is included, and how much does it typically run?
Car payment + Insurance +gas+ parking (campus and apartments potentially)	$400	Is it worth it to have a car where you are going or should you budget subway fare instead?
Airfare or Train Fare	$1000	If you are going out of state, do you plan to fly back for holidays or summers? How many of such trips will you take?
Internet, Cable, Phone	$100	Are you on a family phone plan? Can you get a "bundle" deal or just have internet in your lab? See what you can and can't live without.
Groceries	$200	This is a highly conservative estimate, based off of an estimated target of $50 weekly for groceries. Shopping with a list and for specific recipes can cut down the cost significantly. Eating cheaply doesn't mean eating poorly, just being smart about it!
Eating out	$50	Eventually your fellow grad students may want to eat out, and reserving some money for this can be helpful. Eating out can cost a lot over the long haul, so consider going out for coffee only, lunch, or dessert. For drinkers, keep an eye on the bar tab and, of course, drink in moderation!!

Expense Category	Cost	Considerations
Target/Walmart, etc.	$50	It's always amazing how you walk into Target planning to walk out with toothpaste and come out with six extra "must-have" items. That said, hygiene items can add up, so just have a pre-set limit in mind so you don't buy every new cleanser that comes out.
Gym membership? Yoga?	$60	This can range by region. One of the smartest things to do is using the university's student gym. At Stanford there was a local community yoga and aerobics studio where classes cost only $6 each. Look for deals and steals so you can be healthy without the guilt of a hefty gym membership fee.
Health Insurance	$130	Some graduate student health programs cover more than others. Make sure to see what your coverage is like and also what you must pay out of pocket.
Start up cost?	Varies	Depending on how much "stuff" you already possess and whether or not you end up somewhere furnished, at the beginning there is always a start-up cost to moving anywhere. You will ultimately need disinfecting wipes and toilet bowl cleaner, but you might need a new mattress too. This cost can range, but should be one-time only.
Miscellaneous	$100	It can always be safe to set aside a little bit for the unforeseen costs that may come your way. It may be a flat tire or just a birthday gift. But start setting aside even a small sum for emergencies.

Your Turn!

★ *PhDebt-free: Consider using technology to your advantage for smart financial planning. Two excellent resources include Paycheck City's salary calculator (www.paycheckcity.com) which can give you a sense of* what your take-home pay will look like once state and federal taxes are deducted and Mint.com which can help you budget. Nothing is worse than thinking you have more money than you do and signing the lease on an apartment that will suddenly take more out of your check than you thought. Additionally, CNN's money calculator (http://money.cnn.com/calculator/pf/cost-of-living/) can help you identify the differences in cost of living nationwide. You fill in where you currently live and how much you make and then get to see how much you'd have to make in your new city to have a comparable standard of living. This can be tricky if you are coming straight out of undergrad into grad school. However, it might be able to give you a sense of how far stipends might go in two different states. Maybe one seems too low, but in actuality is set correctly for the region. Other times it really is too low to live off of without a supplemental loan or income. Finally, make a list of "slashable" items. No, we aren't talking scary films. Think about pricier items you might have to let go of to save a little extra while in graduate school. It might be switching from salon shampoo to something found in a retail store. Perhaps cutting out those extra lattes and getting a coffeemaker instead. Every little bit counts!

STUDIO APARTMENT OR WHITE PICKET FENCE?

Close your eyes for a moment and envision your future life in graduate school. What do you see? Are you sitting on a cozy couch in a living room by the fireplace working on problem sets? Are you in a high-efficiency studio apartment overlooking the city? Perhaps you are just miles away from the beach. We all have our own vision of how we'd like the future to look. While we can't control all of it, there are aspects which we can have more say around. Where we live is one of them.

There are many important issues for consideration when thinking about what your graduate school lifestyle will look like. In the previous section, I provided a framework for thinking in a financially savvy way. Where you might live also feeds into this.

For example, in smaller towns it is not uncommon for graduate students to purchase or rent homes during their tenure. After all, they will be there for at least four years, so why not get comfortable? For others, it is all about the cultural opportunities of bigger cities even if it means sacrificing personal space and gaining a roommate to do so. In the end, it all becomes a careful balance. You simply can't have it all, and something will have to give. For example, if being by the beach in San Diego is important to you, it is unrealistic to assume you will be living in a beachfront luxury home minutes from campus. Any amenity to obtain, you have to be fully prepared to pay an arm and a leg for. However, if colder winters or humid summers aren't a problem and small town life suits you, middle America and the South may greet you with open arms.

Now here is something else I learned. Balance is key. As a West Coast girl, I was interested in leaving the West to broaden my horizons metaphorically speaking. And yet, the East Coast seemed like far too big of a change. I found the Midwest was the perfect place for me. It definitely took some adjusting, but the pace and relative ease of life could not be beat for me. I was less than two hours from Chicago if I wanted cultural and artistic stimulation and 40 minutes from the beautiful farmland and lakes of Michigan. The setting was quiet without distractions, which allowed me to get ample work done in little time. In many ways for me and my personality, it was pretty ideal. It gave me the stability and security I was looking for while engaging in a strong intellectually rigorous program.

Being in a smaller town also allowed for more intimate social connections. Over the course of four years I could say my graduate school program and friends in many ways became a second home. That said, location is also important to consider for future career aspirations. For some, where they complete their graduate studies ends up being where they look for a job. Hence four years of solid networking can work to one's advantage. This is less of a help if you are planning to relocate elsewhere.

Curriculums such as those in psychology programs are set up to meet that state's licensure requirements. For example, if I wanted a license in California, I'd be roughly five classes short due to my curriculum in Indiana. I'd be one class short for the state of Washington, and so forth. Further, it is important to think about fellowships and summer programs and how those may feed into ideal locations for your future. For example, while graduate school can be a great time to try out a new region or environment, fellowship and post-graduate training years can be best completed in an area where one would like to settle.

Finally, be sure to consider the social climate of where your program may be located. For example, I came to find that while students in the Bay area had a myriad of cultural and social opportunities to immerse themselves, they often complained of feeling isolated and alone in such a large region. The traffic, hustle, and bustle were too much. However, it is also possible to make connections with graduate student groups to find those smaller circles. But overall, it is important to talk to current graduate students to get a feel of what their lives are like.

During graduate school I lived on campus in graduate student housing. While this meant dealing with roommates (OK, most likely them having to deal with me), our graduate housing community offered events galore. From hot chocolate and cookies before final exams to movie nights, a community garden, weekly summer barbeques, to field trips, many of the good friends and community I built was as a result of my housing community. And frankly the first time in my life when I experienced the shrill sound of those tornado sirens going off, I quickly made my way to the neighbors who coached me through it all. Later on many of those neighbors became best friends. That said, it can be very important to think critically about where and near whom you live.

Your Turn!

★ *PhDirections: As you are considering the locale of your graduate program, don't be afraid to use tools such as Google Maps just to get a lay of the land. Think about the factors that are most important to you. It wasn't until after I'd left my graduate program and lived half a mile away from a Trader Joe's that I found out what a critical element had been missing for me all along. Now I make sure wherever I go, access to amenities such as health foods stores, yoga studios, and affordable but quality housing are available. Don't be shy to do a quick Google search for apartments in cities where your program might be located. Are they driving distance? Do mostly undergraduate students live there? These are all factors to consider.*

SELECTING YOUR MAGIC GENIE…
OR CRUELLA DE VIL

I could probably write an entire book entitled, *Basement Lab Cries: Horror Stories of the Untold*. If it were made into a motion picture, the trailer would be accompanied by spooky music, the kind with the uneasy violins. Okay, this is a bit of an exaggeration. But I will say that some of the worst graduate school "horror stories" that I've heard pertain to the student-advisor match. Often when students think about the notion of "fit" with their advisor, their mind immediately goes to research topics and compatibility. However, there is actually a much more important and different type of compatibility that is too often neglected. This is the student-advisor work and personality style fit. In fact, as I write this, I'm surprised there isn't a widely available inventory or measure to assess for this given its importance. While I'm not suggesting an eHarmony style match with your advisor, it is helpful to gauge what your advisor's work style and expectations are like.

In my first year of graduate school I was struck by the variability inherent in graduate student-advisor relationships. As I'd heard about the advisor who would go out for sushi with students back in undergrad, I assumed most relationships would be fairly informal. However, I came to find quite a range of interactions. For example, there were those advisors who met with students daily or weekly and, to be honest, micromanaged unlike any other. They sent their students four-page single-spaced emails with critiques of everything they had done wrong—just in that one week! There were other advisors who didn't even know if their student was in the country or not. Then there were those that asked their students to babysit their children. You can quickly start to see how it can be confusing to get the lay of the land.

In my case, my advisor was an administrator. For me, this was the perfect arrangement. I saw him monthly in our administrative building and had no lab duties for him, given his position. Sure, I had to schedule meetings with him through his secretary due to his hectic and demanding schedule, but I wasn't burdened with extra tasks or watched like a hawk. Each meeting I typed up two agendas—one for him and one for my records. I'd present every conference I was submitting abstracts to, discuss grants or publications I was working on, and then ask any clarifying questions that were needed. I was able to provide evidence of my full plate through a thorough run down of short and long-term goals and plans. As a self-starter, this was an ideal match for me.

It was a relationship that leaned toward the formal side, but that was still full of warmth and understanding. My advisor trusted me, and this was in effect one of the most meaningful parts of our relationship. He trusted me to test out new ideas, charter unknown seas, and was there when I needed him. He was someone I deeply respected and saw as a fatherly figure.

Granted, in many ways the fates aligned for me to be paired with this particular advisor. I could have also been matched with someone that fit the "young and hip" description of an advisor. Or someone on the "cutting edge of research." But instead, much like my own father, my advisor was wise, calm, full of strength, and support. He was someone who was settled in his career, who had been around long enough to not panic about tenure or push me to run his studies. Although he often suggested novel ideas such as combining mental health with politics and advocacy, he never urged me to do anything. He just suggested ideas for growth like good parents who know how to plant seeds in their children's minds.

In navigating your graduate school years, you will find that your advisor comes to hold many prominent positions in your career and life. They are ultimately the ones who go to bat for you at faculty student review meetings, and are the ones who chair your thesis and dissertation meetings. They help to defend the work you do, and are essentially one of your biggest advocates in your program and/or department. Your advisor may even be the one that finds pockets of money to help fund your study or keep you from taking out a loan for the summer.

However, more than holding professional significance in your life, the relationship with your advisor can impact you for years to come even after your program is completed. Therefore, getting to know your advisor a little bit beyond research logistics is important. We are all human, and all seek understanding and connection. Thus, while it is normal for undergraduates and beginning graduate students to be anxious around or even fear potential or existing advisors, it is important to try to get to know them beyond research and classes. They have a genuine interest in you, and so it is alright to be interested in finding more out about them.

I recall the very first lunch meeting I ever had with my advisor. We met at one of the swanky restaurants on campus and I was a nervous wreck. I was homesick, uncertain if I had whatever "it" was to be a graduate student, and just desperately wanted my advisor to like me. True to my navigationally-challenged roots, I also got a little lost on my way over as if I wasn't panicked enough. I recall speaking at a million miles a minute with maybe a bit too much forced effervescence. He told me to slow down and implicitly to calm down. In fact, in my earliest of meetings with my advisor I recall my frustration at his repeated statement to me to slooooooow dooowwwn. And yet not just in the field of psychology, but any field, this is one of the most valuable lessons we can learn—to slow down, let the process happen and unfold naturally, to not force things.

Certainly it took some time to figure out what my relationship with my advisor was exactly like. Each graduate student I was friends with seemed to have such markedly different experiences. Over the years I've heard of graduate students who would break down into tears during or after lab meetings. Others would develop depressive symptoms after obtaining feedback from their advisors. Part of the rollercoaster analogy I so often use with graduate student clients comes from ups and downs experienced that are related to advisors. Your experiment is going well, your advisor is happy with you, and you're at the top of the world. Something goes wrong, your advisor throws a bunch of work on your plate on a limited timeline and you're at rock bottom. Trying to cultivate a healthy and balanced relationship where you can also respectfully assert your needs can be your greatest asset. Often times I recall worrying about meeting certain departmental requirements, or something wasn't going well elsewhere in my program. Talking it out with my advisor nearly always helped. He had solutions, ideas, and encouragement which is really what all grad students need at the end of the day.

Aside from the support advisors often provide with respect to academia, they are also a great support for getting through graduate school. Regardless of whether they are junior faculty or have been out of graduate school for a decade, many remember their own experiences acutely. They recall the challenges of their statistics sequences, and struggling to make their mark in the research world. If they had clinical training, they may even remember their first clients and experiences. Many advisors are more than willing to empathize and share the struggles they endured when they see you in need of emotional support as well. While we may be tempted to put on our battalion armor every time we walk into our advisor's offices, attempting to appear calm and collected at all times, this really is not necessary. Of course, we should also avoid regularly emptying their Kleenex boxes, but a little bit of vulnerability only shows you are human too. Thus, don't be afraid to seek academic *and* emotional support from advisors.

While the protégé model of student-advisorial matches have fallen somewhat out of style, a major advantage of having an advisor is gaining valuable insight into your future career. Many advisors may come to hold additional responsibilities within a university such as being a departmental chair, a dean, or even a vice provost. While in some cases such factors may modify the amount of time you are able to spend with them, in other cases this can allow you a sneak peek of sorts into life as an administrator, coordinator, and other roles.

As many students enter graduate school claiming a life ambition of being an academic or scholar, by the end of four to five years sometimes this just is not an ideal career match anymore for a number of reasons. Some come to acquire families and have to budget their time, while for others their interests may change. However, advisors can usually offer a wealth of information on different types of jobs, post-docs, and other such positions. Being open, and honest with them, and having a candid discussion of where you see yourself professionally will provide you with untold benefits and far fewer sleepless nights!

A few final notes related to finding an advisor involve seeking out information from current graduate students. While some prospectives may doubt the accuracy of reports given by current graduate students, I will say that one can be clever and find ways of reading in between the lines. For example, are advisor switches common in the department? Are they discouraged? Why do they occur? Also, how many students has the advisor graduated in the time they have been there? It wasn't until halfway through my program that I started noticing how some faculty members had only graduated one student during their tenure or none at all. Their previous graduate students had switched to other advisors. This is key and very telling information.

Also, while I was highly fortunate to find a solid advisor, I found graduate student attitudes around advisor permanence varied. For example, some believed they had to "suck it up" with advisors just because this had been the initial arrangement. They were fearful of rocking the boat or hurting feelings. Others felt more empowered and made switches to new advisors with tact and strength. Making sure your needs are getting met is extremely important and something to prioritize. The handful of highly intelligent and capable graduate students who I've seen prematurely terminate their programs often did so largely because of adversarial relationships with advisors. Some didn't feel supported. Others lost motivation. If I had to make a guess, I'd say open and honest communication with their advisors could have had them walking out with much more.

I recall in my moments of uncertainty during graduate school I sometimes thought of my "back up degree plan." In many graduate programs a master's degree is awarded after a thesis project or completion of oral exams at the end of the second year. It is helpful to know what the rules are because in the event your Ph.D. program really isn't working out for you, it is helpful to know you can exit with a Master's degree. So many students go through years of work, only to later drop out, without much to show for it. The idea of knowing you can get the Master's (and perhaps avoid advertising you are planning to exercise this option) is great peace of mind. In moments when I had the existential "what am I doing with my life" dilemma, I always reminded myself that I could leave at any moment. And, I'd have a Master's degree from Notre Dame to boot. While that day didn't come, anything you can say to yourself to obtain inner peace is tremendously helpful.

It is also beneficial to remember that at the end of the day, your advisor really is your advocate. To this day when I make certain career choices, I think about my advisor and how he would respond or what his advice would be. I remember not only his poise and class, but also his belief in social justice and the greater good. I think about how I can use myself as a vehicle toward helping others. Surely I'm no clone of my advisor and our approaches may at times differ. But in heart, our values overlap significantly. Having a respectful and strong relationship with your advisor really does impact you for years to come.

Your Turn!

★ *PhDamage-Control: Although at times you may feel desperate just to get into a graduate program, resist the desire to throw yourself into an arrangement that could later backfire. Challenge yourself to reach out to current graduate students to learn about various advisors in the department. Figure out if students ever have a "co-advisor" situation and how this came about. Don't be afraid to ask the tough questions. Don't feel the need to obtain excessive amount of information or take everything at face value. However, do exercise your own good judgment and trust your gut instincts.*

THE MINDSET OF A BUDDHA

Once you've wholeheartedly determined that a Ph.D. program is your next step in life, it can help to run that old Spice Girls song in your head. "I'll tell you what I want what I really really want." If the second half happens to say, "I wanna, I wanna,

I wanna, I wanna, I wanna really really really wanna get a Ph.D. ha," then you're definitely on the right track. Or at the very least you are laughing at this allusion, and that works too. And yet, this leads seamlessly into one of my final points for this chapter and section. The process of applying to, interviewing for, and accepting an offer into a graduate program is a significant life decision that can feel taxing at times. Taking care of your well-being should never take a back seat in the entirety of this process. It can be tempting to cast aside needed workouts, healthy eating, and social time to apply to one more school or study for that GRE section one last time. The process of applying has a timeline that can be seen as infinite—no true beginning or end, just endless and everlasting. Therefore it will be important to exercise self-control and limits.

Remember that applying to graduate school really is like a full-time job. If you look back to the sample schedule draft I've provided, you'll notice in my final year I was taking a minimal number of courses, and most of them were taken "Pass/Fail." This was because I knew in advance that I'd be traveling across the country, changing time zones back and forth and would likely be missing classes. I took a lighter load, and it was still challenging to do it all. Some of the most well-balanced graduate students I've met actually applied to graduate school after taking a minimum of one year off from school.

The lesson to be learned is to take it easy and be kind to yourself. And have a sense of humor. Create a solid Plan B that doesn't sound disappointing. While ideally you will get into a graduate program or the one of your choice, if it doesn't happen the first time, it isn't the end of the world even if it feels like it. Whether it's completing a Master's degree program that is financially feasible and a strong program, doing extra research, or even pursuing side interests, come up with alternatives in the event things don't work out exactly as you'd like.

Throughout this book I will return time and again to the importance of self-care wherever you are in the process. Much like preventive health care, it is a means of keeping things from going awry rather than putting a band-aid on a dam later on. So start thinking about coping mechanisms and what they look like. What do you typically do in times of stress or uncertainty? Some seek spiritual guidance and solace, others go for a massage. Some may bake away their stressors in the form of muffins and others reach out to friends. Watching funny films helps others. Come up with a self-care plan. The Ph.D. isn't the only thing you are planning for. You are also planning for success and support throughout the process.

Your Turn!

★ *PhDiary: Research has shown that one's subjective well-being (happiness) can be impacted by tuning into gratitude. Start adopting an "attitude of gratitude" and list three things you are grateful for each and every day before you go to bed at night. Write them down and keep an ongoing list. Evidence shows this can significantly boost your wellness. When engaging in the challenging process of applying to graduate school, keeping an inner sense of calm and gratitude can help!*

Part II

Primping: Graduate School (Years 1-3)

CHAPTER 4

WALKING ALONG THE IVY-COVERED BUILDINGS

"No one has the ability to make you feel inferior without your consent."
—Eleanor Roosevelt

GETTING OFF THE FLOOR, THEN CLIMBING THE LADDER

My first year of graduate school was actually kind of a nightmare. I was plagued by anxiety, worry, homesickness, and, frankly, a sense of panic. What had I done? I'd never lived away from my family or even done my own laundry. I didn't know how to cook, clean, and certainly didn't know what to do in the event of a severe thunderstorm warning and tornado watch. In time, I made it. But it felt like the longest year of my life.

Early on (and still to this day), I remember being awe-struck by the beauty of the Notre Dame campus. I was amazed that I'd even made it there. As I walked the paths along lush trees and blooming flowerbeds past the Gothic-style regal buildings, I was unsure how I was going to do it all. I, a 22-year old West Coast girl, was going to spend the next four years attempting to get a Ph.D., from a well-respected university no less. What had I gotten myself into?

As the excitement and nervousness of orientation wore off, I didn't know what to do with myself. Fortunately, uncertain of what electives I should be taking, I signed up for one fewer class than my peers. And it made a tremendous difference. I was already treading water slowly, no need to jump into the deep end. It's somewhat endearing now when I think back to those days, but it all felt devastating back then. I didn't know anyone or what to do, and, frankly, I missed my family too. A lot. Deciding I'd try my best, I did what I dubbed the "efficient mope and cry." I'd fold laundry, a few tears streaming down my face. I'd do the dishes, still crying. Vacuum, still crying.

In retrospect, I probably should have gone to therapy. But I also knew I was adjusting. It was an enormous shift not only in my life, but also my identity. The problem with being in clinical psychology sometimes is having an acute awareness of diagnosis and impairment criteria. In my head, I was still getting A's in stats lab and attending all my classes with good performance. So long as my mood was not affecting my main mission, I'd be fine, I rationalized. That said, I also shared a gnawing thought that so many graduate student women share. Maybe I should drop out. It's a thought that countless women come to share. Some have revealed it is a thought they had every single day of graduate school for several years. A fighter by nature though, I devised a Plan B. And also a Plan C and Plan D.

Plan B: when thoroughly depressed, take the bus, go the mall and see if you still want to drop out of school. This sounds ridiculous at the outset, I know. But often just being out of the school environment, near the familiar sights and sounds that were also comforting back home was enough to do the trick. I'd chitchat with the salespeople and sometimes I'd watch the live feed from Huntington Beach at the Hollister store. Something about seeing the Pacific Standard Time reading made me feel better. Even the sharp scent of overpowering men's cologne wafting out of Abercrombie reminded me of home, as the smell of Fierce is pretty universal.

Plan C: go to therapy. Yes, I know what you were thinking. Seriously, she was going to discount that option? I did go in for an intake session for an outside therapy referral just in case at one point early in graduate school. Knowing that if I needed to talk there would be someone there to listen was helpful. I also enlisted the help of family and friends back home as my confidantes and mini-therapists-on-call.

Plan D: get your Master's degree and leave. My friends and I still joke about this. I was going to get a degree one way or another. Even if I didn't walk out with the Ph.D., at some point, you need to just cut your losses and move on.

Plan E: (I know you weren't expecting this one!) take a leave. Graduate programs often offer medical leaves and personal leaves. I toyed with the idea that if I really wanted to go home at any time, I could. Eventually after a month on mom's couch, I'd probably get bored and want to come back to school.

In times when I was really down, I told myself something simple—you know where your suitcases are, and you have enough in your savings to buy a ticket home. Whenever you want to leave, you can pack up and do so. Allowing myself the freedom to leave at any point in time was perhaps one of the most empowering thoughts I had throughout graduate school. And it was the truth. No one was making me stay. It was my personal decision. When I decided that a degree in psychology was no longer what I wanted, I could simply leave. Usually when I talked to myself in this way, my solution was clear. No, I didn't need to read all 250 pages of that psychopathology reading with painstaking attention to detail. I could just read the abstracts, intros, discussions, and skim the rest. If it was truly a disaster in class the next day, I could re-evaluate my situation. But that day never came.

Back when I lectured at Stanford, one of our guest speakers for a class I taught was the dean of the graduate school. He would come in and give our undergraduate crisis counselors a primer on graduate students and common concerns. It was "Graduate Students 101" if you will. What was most striking about his talk was at the very beginning. He asked undergraduates what their first week of classes was like. It usually involved a "welcome week" of sorts, RAs and staff to welcome them to their dorms, help them find classes and so forth.

Graduate students on the other hand trickle in all throughout the summer. They arrive by themselves usually with a lone suitcase looking completely lost. I realized this wasn't an exaggeration when, one day outside of my yoga class held in the graduate student commons area, I was approached by these very first-year graduate students asking me where they could check-in for their housing assignments.

It's true, graduate students often don't have someone to greet them and welcome them to their new home for the next several years. As a result, the tendency can be to jump in head-first just to get acquainted and a sense of normalcy. But there is nothing wrong with starting off slowly. You don't have to spend your entire first day in your new lab trying to figure out what to do with yourself. Go home, take your orientation packets and actually read them. Find out about health insurance, your student counseling center, student groups you can join, and exactly what your program requirements are. Many Ph.D. programs can have vastly different requirement and these may even change from year to year. As such, those early documents are the ones to store in a safe place. They were the binding documents or even contracts of what was required of us in the program. So when a few years later a new requirement appeared out of thin air, we could refer back to our entering documents and find a way to save us from unnecessary headaches later on.

Your Turn!

★ *PhDebut: As you make your debut into graduate school, it's important to do one simple thing. Take a deep breath. Your emotions may run from excited and thrilled to terrified and anxious. It's the very beginning of that emotional rollercoaster. But the good news is that if you slow down to assess all that is going on around you, it can give you time to adjust and figure out what you need to do. So maybe take a leisurely walk around campus without trying to find your way to a meeting. Just allow yourself to take it all in. It might sound cliché, but go the bookstore. Maybe get yourself a new school mug or sweatshirt. Welcome and congratulate yourself on your arrival.*

PHDIVAS-IN-TRAINING AND SKULLETTES

The earliest weeks of graduate school are also an excellent time to figure out the game plan for the remainder of your academic career. As one may already be so overwhelmed by taking in all the information and figuring out the next few days to weeks, it can be easy to neglect the big picture. One of the best things to do may be to find a mini-mentor or PhDiva-in-Training. I recall looking up to one of our graduate students who was two years ahead of me when I arrived. We had colleagues back home in common, but more than that she was one of those star graduate students one would look up to. For me anyway, it wasn't that she was on some superstar fellowship, but rather that she was upbeat, friendly, and always ahead of the game. So one day I asked to meet with her for coffee. Over time she became one of my best resources, mentors, and a friend. Not only did I learn the tips and tricks no one ever tells you about, but I also learned how to time my progress through the program.

As someone very motivated to complete my Ph.D. in a timely manner, I came to figure out that with four research benchmarks in four years (first-year project, thesis, quals, and dissertation), I'd need to average more than one project a year to finish in the time I desired. Later, I figured exactly how to plan things out to save some major time (discussed further in this section). However, I wouldn't have known in the first place that I needed to speed things up unless I'd actually spoken to someone a few years ahead of me.

Furthermore, reaching out to fellow women is a wonderful way of not only networking but also brainstorming. It was through my friendships with women that I thought about places to apply for internship, different career options, research ideas, and more. It was also through these women that I was able to give and receive support. When I was in my second year of graduate school I recall many amazing women in the entering class who I befriended. Many were dissatisfied with the lack of mentorship and guidance outside of the formal academic advisors. For many who go to professional schools such as those in medicine, law, and business, the murkiness of graduate school is quite difficult to explain unless you've been in it. There are things to accomplish with little insight into exactly how one goes about it all. Learning and sharing from networks of women is one of the best ways of accomplishing this.

At one point during graduate school I finally saw the feature film, Skulls, about a Yale secret society full of intrigue and adventures. As a joke I suggested to a few of my close female friends in graduate school that we create our own women's secret society and dub it the "Skullettes." After a film viewing party of our group's namesake, our own unofficial group formed. Of course, there were no death-defying hazing rituals, nor secret events, or hoods and cloaks. And the group formally met for maybe a year. But what we found was a group of women to laugh and cry with. On too many occasions we had thought we were going through our doubts and worries alone. When we allowed ourselves to be vulnerable and open up, we realized how much strength we could find in ourselves and each other.

Your Turn!

★ *PhDyads and More: Think about reaching out to one or more women in the department to start building your new network. One of the most valuable therapy "assignments" I often gave to graduate students was to reach out and share their struggle with one trusted person. They were always shocked! Although they feared seeming "weak" or being judged, they often found others felt the same. Whether it's forming a group or just coffee with one other person, just be mindful that it not turn into a full-blown vent session that leaves you feeling worse. Maybe limit it to 10 minutes of complaining and another 30 minutes of figuring out how to actually improve the situation.*

HARNESS YOUR SUPERPOWERS

One of my favorite groups to work with when I worked as a university counseling center therapist was graduate students. This was due to many reasons. Their readiness and maturity to really self-reflect as well as their dedication to growth was a really fun part of working with them. Sometimes though, they came to see me at the very end—when they were getting kicked out of their department or were suddenly experiencing panic attacks. One commonality among many of these student was a lack of strategies geared toward self-care and coping. Often times I'd turn to these students and ask them what their usual coping strategies were in the face of stressors. They'd look at me with blank expressions on their faces. Coping mechanisms? What are those?! Of course many of us have a working knowledge of what that might mean for others. What I found to be common was students not having a readily available list of what they would look like for themselves.

I often explained coping mechanisms to students simply as follows, "When you get stressed or upset, what are some of the things that calm you down?" Once I removed "going to a bar… drinking…" as an option and students began to think about it, their ideas would flow more freely. "Go for a run….bake cookies….call my mom….talk to my boyfriend…journal….listen to music…paint…play my guitar….pray at church." What's important to realize is that coping mechanisms can also look different depending on where you are. For example, while at Notre Dame, much of my coping involved going for runs around the lakes, lighting a candle at the grotto, or visiting the basilica and saying a prayer. In this type of environment, all those options were available to me.

Flash forward to my time at Berkeley. There was no grotto, no lakes to run around, and certainly no basilica. So my coping mechanisms had to shift. There, yoga was more accessible as was great lavender gelato and lots of movie theatres. If there was ever a year in my life when I was finally current on films, it was probably that year. Anything that was walking distance was fair game, so that meant lots of movies and yummy foods. The next year at Stanford my landscape changed again. This time I became more dedicated to a community yoga studio, reading books for leisure, lighting scented candles, and going to Target. Yes, Target. It was within walking distance of where I lived and so whenever the going got rough, I got going to Target. The best part is that I can now walk into any Target store across the country and tell you exactly where you can find any item you might need with amazing speed and precision.

The overarching point being that one needs to have in visible sight a solid list of activities that can help in shifting one's mood when facing difficult challenges. For me, a difficult or challenging time usually means first trying to talk it out with family and friends. Next on the list is usually going to a yoga studio, going for a walk or hike, a long shower, and maybe writing, reading, cleaning, baking and any number of activities. Again, over time my own list may look very different. I may become a Zumba fanatic and decide that is my go-to. Either way be sure to acknowledge that circumstances change and we change. For example a busy mom may have more difficulty physically removing herself from the situation if she is the only one at home with the children. But maybe soothing classical music, and aromatherapy candles can help for a bit.

Your Turn!

★ *PhDe-Stress: Come up with a nifty list of coping mechanisms and have it available in plain sight to refer to when needed. Often if you wait to come up with the list when you are already feeling agitated, it won't necessarily spark the creative juices and nothing will seem satisfying. When annoyed you might not even want to do anything on the list. But you know yourself best. Come up with those surefire tactics that always make you feel better. Comedy television show re-runs, chamomile tea, and some Ben & Jerry's anyone?*

TWEED AND SWEATS AREN'T THE ONLY OPTIONS

In the first section of this book I made a nod toward some of the more offensive advice I'd heard about in similar graduate school guides for women. Some involved direct recommendations of what women "should" and "shouldn't" wear. It reminded me of Victorian era etiquette guides. I would argue there are no hard and fast rules regarding attire and that in the academy you will see a little bit of everything. This doesn't mean I'd recommend emulating exactly what you see donned by professors or fellow students. Hence, you are not limited to tweed or sweats. Or dramatic scarves, excessive handcraft fair jewelry, or jeans from the early '90s (or '80s in some cases).

I would suggest some basic factors to consider. First off, who are you and what makes you feel comfortable? In graduate school I saw it all—the slightly disheveled sweats all day look and the girls with their perfect skirts, heels, and shawls. I didn't exactly belong to either category. After all, I spent the first year of graduate school exclusively wearing what was nicknamed my periwinkle "sleeping bag coat," which effectively served as an excellent shield against Midwestern winter weather. But once my body began to adjust to the temperature and I had to see therapy clients, my attire needed to approach "professional" or "smart business casual," whatever that means exactly. I came to realize that dressing professionally didn't have to mean dumping what little you had left of your stipend check into lots of expensive outfits. Sure, I had to come up with something better than jeans and t-shirts, but I figured out that even nice fitted jeans in a darker wash could be multi-purpose. With a nice blazer and nice footwear (not sneakers) and maybe a necklace, I could make it work. In fact, I saved a lot of money by going with neutral colors that could be mixed and matched with various tops and bottoms of staple colors that weren't going to go out of style anytime soon (brown, navy, black). Accessories helped to make things a little less boring.

When helping one of my best friends and colleagues move, I once helped out with the closet portion. I counted an impressive collection of roughly 30 cardigans in a rainbow of colors. It was her style, and the occasional brightly colored cardigan helped her achieve professional and fun. As such, it's not necessary to find the Cosmo version of graduate school fashion. Insider tip: some of the best-dressed ladies I came across in graduate school actually purchased much of their wardrobe from Target! They knew exactly which items to pick that looked ultra chic.

For the fashion enthusiasts, you certainly don't need my tips and already have a sense of what does and doesn't work for you. But I would share that sometimes being too fashion forward can backfire. I'm not saying this is fair or even OK. I recall going to a teaching seminar led by a women who explained that women historically get lower teacher ratings than men almost without fail regardless of whether or not they employ identical methods and mannerisms. Her point was that students (females included) expect men to be experts. As such, the nuances matter less. It doesn't matter what the male professor looks like when he comes up to give a lecture. Women on the other hand aren't afforded that luxury. If she's under-dressed, then she is "frumpy." If she is over-dressed, she is "trying too hard" or even worse, "skanky." I'd always say err on the side of what works for you rather than any persona you are trying to put on. So please don't don "smart people glasses" if your vision is just fine. I found that for me blazers and collared shirts made me feel fresher and more composed and so that's what I went with. That may not work for everyone.

Although I cringe to have to say it, ladies, I do have one hard and fast rule regarding professional attire that is relatively easy to remember: under no circumstances should you wear anything you might wear to a nightclub into lab or the office. I know this sounds ridiculous and obvious, but you'd be surprised. I can often immediately tell at professional conferences who the undergraduate women are and who the graduate students are simply off of this rule. A lot of women come with extremely short and tight skirts, stilettos, and low-cut tops. While undergraduates sometimes get away with this under the "they don't know any better" rule, I sometimes worry that not everyone gets the memo that this isn't the best choice of attire. As for animal prints, less is more. Trust me on this one!

Your Turn!

★ *PhDress: Dress to impress... yourself. Go online and peruse some of your favorite "professional" fashion stores. Look at the outfits they put together and get a sense of what you'd like for yourself. Again, the idea isn't to copy an image or become someone you're not. But most of us have those stores whose collections we admire. Figure out how to do it for less, or shop their clearance and on-sale items. Start building up that professional wardrobe, while keeping in mind that Rome wasn't built in a day. Start with one pair of nice pants, blazer, or multi-purpose work dress. Before you know it, you won't have to look in your closet horrified that you don't have anything for that department banquet or meeting with the chair.*

HONING YOUR INNER RESEARCH WONDER WOMAN

While one of my aims in this book is to certainly encourage women to be efficient, direct, and save time and energy when feasible, I do want to emphasize that this only works when one is putting in the time and effort in the first place. To climb to the top, you have to be very knowledgeable and well-informed about your field. This doesn't mean you have to take a conventional way to get there, but it does mean you need to work hard. For starters, this means not comparing yourself to others. By being your own greatest competitor, you won't be distracted by others, or limiting yourself by their definition of "excellence." What I would suggest is figuring out a reasonable means of becoming very well-read in your specific field, but also overlapping domains.

At the outset, this can sound over-whelming, but it need not be. If you started reading this book during your undergraduate years, then you may have already known to start joining professional organizations, attending conferences and becoming immersed in the world of academia. If not, it's certainly not too late. I'd recommend working daily at becoming well-versed in your field through easy steps. For example, during graduate school I had an innate interest in feminist psychology and the media. So I joined those organizations for fun, but also perused their journals during breakfast. This didn't mean I had to read every single article, but I often skimmed the abstracts and discussion sections just to get a sense of the various topics. I also subscribed to two more general national organizational bodies. While I read some of their articles, I also learned to read their magazines which provided short "user-friendly" synopses of the very same articles published in their journals. I often read these magazines on flights, when a client didn't show up for a session, or other free time. Meaning, I didn't obsess about getting to everything, but I managed to cover a whole lot more ground than if I hadn't been reading at all. Further, once I began writing for Psychology Today, I wound up spending ample time on their website while checking obsessively to see how many hits my articles had gotten. As I scrolled through their pages, the works of colleagues and experts in the field caught my eye and soon enough I was reading psychology literature briefs for fun! After all, I was in this field because of my intrinsic interests.

What happens all too often for women pursuing higher education is that they become so bogged down by the daily mundane details of research or coursework, that their inherent passions start to die down. They are so overwhelmed by uninteresting tasks that their motivation quickly goes down. Keeping your head above water enough to look at the beautiful landscape around you can provide a quick re-charge and reminder of what you're doing in the field. It can also open up new exciting areas of inquiry to explore.

Also, think about finding a way to set yourself apart, to be at the top of your game. Picture it in your mind. What would this look like? For me, it meant getting a few grants I was interested in, but also making a larger public contribution. However, coming into graduate school I had a decent amount of publications. Instead of taking it as a sign to "relax," I used this as an opportunity to find other unique ways of tapping into other talents. So while public blogging was uncommon for a graduate student (two faculty in my department were also experts for the same site), it allowed me to find my own way to shine.

Your Turn!

★ *PhDominate: Take out some paper now. List off what it would take for you to start to feel like an expert in your field. Put those feelings of self-doubt aside—there is no room for them here. It's just you and your dreams. Now, take a look at that list and figure out what it would take for each of those steps to occur. Remember that confidence is built step by step. So start laying down that foundation strongly!*

YOU CAN'T PLEASE THEM ALL, BUT SOME COUNT MORE THAN OTHERS

The advisor in graduate school is (as you can tell by now) someone that is a major determinant of graduate school quality of life. But as often is true with hype, there is also a lot of exaggeration to it. Many talk about advisors in ways that bring horror movie images to mind. They are dictators, mentally unstable, ruthless, on and on. Having been blessed with one of the best around, I will still say that it also involves an ability to learn to adapt to your advisor's style, within reason. For example, with my advisor I was highly anxious my first few years of working with him. I didn't know what to say, how to say it or why he had even chosen me to work with him. Furthermore, he was a high-ranking administrator at the university. Needless to say, my walk from our old three-story psychology building across the quad to the large stately Main Building with the Virgin Mary towering overhead made the word intimidating an understatement. It was like an awkward first meeting with someone you knew was well-intentioned but couldn't quite click with because you were so anxious and busy wondering if your shoes were over or under-dressy.

I came to find that speaking points, in the form of an agenda, were my godsend (and who knows, maybe it was Mary working her magic). But having items to discuss helped make our meetings both productive and informative. It maximized my limited time with my advisor while also allowing me to reap his professional and personal wisdom. Oddly, I've found that with each year that passed, his method in working with me made more and more sense. I recall early on being terrified that he wasn't giving me enough direction or telling me what to do. But as a conscientious student who was handing him agendas, I'm sure he knew I'd be just fine and that that was what I really needed.

Now let's flash to other working styles. Yup, it's the one that is most often typecast as the dictator. It is the micro-manager who is often seeking tenure. They have a dozen projects, minimal experience advising, and have had few graduate students matriculate through the program. While their research is inspired and on the cutting edge, their method may be far from it. Of course they need to start somewhere and someone will have to be their first graduate student. And surely it can be you. But learning limits and your rights is immensely important. You don't want to turn into the students who I mentioned previously. The ones in graduate school for seven years with no funding, and now volunteering to work for free, with no end in sight.

The unfortunate truth is that no one will advocate for you and your timely degree completion other than yourself. So many students are terrified of the outcome of asking for more clarity, saying no to their advisor, or worse, switching their advisors. They remain victims needlessly and accept this fate. Women are particularly prone to this as we are so often taught to be the mediators, that being assertive is not attractive or too "masculine." The question to be asking ourselves is "would a man put up with this?" I was at a graduate student union meeting one time when the issue of stipends came up. Never mind the fact that other disciplines made thousands more than us in psychology, but they actually got raises. My co-representative and I looked at each other with shock and then out into the sea of mostly male faces at the meeting. Even funding that is so often presented as non-negotiable is flexible. In fact, one tidbit most graduate students miss is how much really is negotiable in graduate school. Certainly there are rules and regulations. You can't expect to graduate without coursework or research, but even some courses can be petitioned to be substituted with something else, and other research projects can meet the requirements for different benchmarks.

Many women are often afraid of the idea of petitions, even filing grievances. If they stand out in any noticeable way they may feel they are already standing on thin ice. Why rock the boat, they think to themselves. But all these small instances of "letting it go" here and there add up and are often what lead women to feel fed up and then to pack up and go home. I often think about it in this way. If getting into graduate school in the first place means you have all the necessary tools to graduate, then why not do it? And why not do it in a way that is meaningful, engaging, and inspiring? After all, it's not the marines. It's just graduate school.

Your Turn!

★ *PhDeclaration: Decide right here and right now who the key players are in your academic journey and what you can do to cultivate strong relationships. Determine your communication and work styles and don't be afraid to stand up for your needs. Remember to stay confident and not over-stress about what everyone else is thinking about your performance. Be true to yourself and do your very best. That's all anyone can ask for.*

CHAPTER 5

WHO AM I AND
HOW DID I GET HERE?

"Iris, in the movies, we have leading ladies and we have the best friend.
You, I can tell, are the leading lady, but for some reason,
you're behaving like the best friend."

—*The Holiday*

PERFECTION ISN'T EVERYTHING

My friends from graduate school and I joke still that I spent the first two years of graduate school at home. This is mostly true. To my credit, I was also the first person in my cohort to propose and defend my Master's thesis. I had finished my coursework and fundamental clinical rotations. So by third year, I was ready to go. I found friends, started exercising, and pretty much had a well-rounded and balanced life (as much as one in graduate school can be). I'll get more into these topics in later chapters. My primary purpose in this chapter is to lay out some of the perfectionistic pitfalls and cognitions that can often trip up graduate students.

One of the best pieces of advice I learned early on was from a PhDiva-in-Training to whom I looked up. She was one of those people who made things look effortless, though we all knew how hard she worked. She was respected, and in my eyes most important, was timely. This student was not the sort of girl to dawdle. She completed her program requirements in four years and was on internship by the fifth year. Her brilliant insight passed down to her from her advisor and on to me: no project in graduate school will be your pièce de resistance. Accept it early, internalize it, and move on. This bit of advice also ranks as some of the best I received.

Learning that your many research hurdles are not meant to define your career (that's what post-doc is for) is very freeing. Yes, it is nice to publish and have a program of research. But again, the goal is not to be the departmental superstar. It is to get your requirements done and move on! Trust me, it sounds harsh, but consider this my tough love approach to you, the reader, who is very deserving of a Ph.D. as hassle-free as they come.

In my graduate program, I had four major research benchmarks to clear. By being efficient and realistic, rather than coming up with lofty goals that would keep me around for years, I actually saved myself anywhere from one to three years time toward degree completion. The first project my program required was called the "First-Year Project." It would culminate with a 10-minute PowerPoint to be presented at the beginning of second year in front of the entire faculty and students of the department at large. Intimidating yes, but 10 minutes, no Q&A, and no written portion or anything else to turn in.

Many students used pre-existing data sets from their advisors large lab samples and portioned out a small section to analyze. I was not in a lab. I could have jumped the gun and decide to collect original data. This would have taken much time in getting IRB approval, participants, coding, analyzing. For one year, it was a tall order. Fortunately, there was no rule indicating the data had to be original. Hence, I used my own archival data. As a senior in college I'd received a grant to study multicultural aspects of….wait for it….perfectionism! Being extra aware of the drawbacks of perfectionistic thinking, I received permission from my advisor to go through with the plan. It saved many headaches and much time. The result: my first hurdle was over!

Second task: Master's thesis. This likely was the most challenging study I conducted in graduate school, including my dissertation. But the thesis is really a learning exercise. Through it you learn an incredible amount and are better prepared for your dissertation. If you have not heard it before, allow me to be the first to say it. The Master's thesis proposal and defense are often more difficult for students than their dissertations. Much of it has to do with the learning curve. It involves picking the right committee, not biting off more than you can chew, selecting a topic that is novel, but not too limiting either. The one aspect I am grateful for is that I did my data collection online which made sampling my underserved population a bit easier. I still had a pretty huge study attrition rate, but with many emails, and lots of prayer, the study was completed. My biggest mistake in the whole process? Probably during the defense when I was explaining scale internal consistency and, in a moment of sheer honesty, said I'd just Googled the concept the previous night. The lesson here is even if you do use Google for preparation, please don't announce it.

For many programs, an intermediate step between the Master's defense and dissertation proposal are candidacy, orals, or qualifying exams. Different programs have varying structures, requirements, and names for it. My third research hurdle was actually a choice between two projects for our preliminary exam. I could either take a two- day written test on all the material I had learned throughout graduate school, or write a literature review with intent for publication.

I was in luck, as I'd started a literature review my first year of graduate school as a final project. Naturally enjoying the writing process (and narcissistically loving to see my name in print), I independently refined the paper and submitted it for publication. I will say I went against my professor's advice in that I submitted it to a lower-tiered journal. Frankly, I just wanted a publication and did not have patience for the eternal revise and resubmit dance of prestigious journals. My paper was one that I was passionate about, and one that the literature was in need of, as it pertained to an underserved population. The paper was accepted for publication and I was working on final revisions around the same time I was getting ready for my preliminary exam. It did not make logical sense to me to write another literature review when clearly I'd already written a paper that was publishable, as it was being published. I also had no desire to take a comprehensive written exam. As such, I petitioned the faculty to allow me to use my pre-existing paper to fulfill this requirement. As faculty do want students to matriculate through the program in a timely fashion, believe it or not, they accepted my petition. This easily saved me a year of extra time in my program. Otherwise, I would have had to complete my Master's thesis and preliminary exams in the same year. Add teaching duties, clinical work, and courses, and it was the perfect setup for a mental breakdown. But with some creativity and guts to use what I already had, I effectively became my own biggest advocate.

The dissertation stage, contrary to graduate student lore, is the best part! It is what you have been looking forward to (no, not dreading!) since your first year. You knew it was coming and wondered if you'd even be around to see the day when you'd open up a Word document and save it with the word "dissertation" in the title. Often the excitement and anticipation is cast aside and quickly supplanted by anxiety. There is no reason for this. If you made it past the Master's defense relatively well, there should be no rationale for suddenly deciding you are the most incompetent graduate student in the department. And yet this happens over and over. Each graduate student creates a mental list of every horror story dating 10 years back of each time someone did not pass or almost did not pass. They neglect the details (i.e., this person was not prepared and went against their advisor's advice to defend) and immediately assume they will be the next fatality.

Take that thought, place it in a hot air balloon, and watch it float far, far away. That type of thinking does not help, and, unfortunately, often takes away from the pleasure of realizing you are on the cusp of joining the academy.

In the dissertation phase, there are many things that can command our attention simultaneously. By learning from your past mistakes, you can streamline things. For example, during my dissertation I decided to take advantage of lab research assistants. I interviewed four undergraduates and not having the heart to turn anyone away (I only needed two), invited them all to take part in my data collection. It ended up working fairly well overall, and saved me from figuring out dictation software and transcription. It also earned them credit, research experience, poster presentations, and a letter of recommendation writer, so I'd call it a pretty fair trade overall.

I will admit, though, that there were certainly moments of self-doubt. My dissertation idea was one I'd come up with two years prior. I wondered if this would not be solid enough, because surely a third-year graduate student is not supposed to have "advanced" ideas. But instead of ruminating on it, I presented it to my advisor who approved it and we were off. I recall from my Master's thesis work feeling somewhat insecure that my fellow colleagues were often bogged down in digesting "the literature." Wondering if I wasn't doing enough (and yes, that comparison was already a mistake), I decided this was a dissertation. Of course I must know everything about my topic. And so I printed off roughly 200 pages worth of articles. Now to read them. Preoccupied with anxiety, and going through a weird phase where I kept fantasizing about living in San Diego (surely San Diego Ph.D. candidates live the good life, I thought) I wound up poolside. That's right. I convinced two of my girlfriends that the best way to be productive and get in some playtime (which was exceedingly rare), was to bring our empirical articles to the pool. It was there that over the course of several weeks I read all of the articles that I'd printed out the summer before I proposed my dissertation that fall. It was one of the best ideas I'd had all of graduate school. How ironic it sounds that the moment I decided to loosen-up, things fell into place more.

Your Turn!

★ *PhDitching: Ditch those self-defeating thoughts and perfectionistic thinking. In psychology, we often refer to the type of thinking underlying perfectionism as "must-abatory." Eliminate the words "must" "ought" and "should" from your vocabulary. Replace them with "it would be better if," or "I'd prefer." Just easing up on your language can ease things in your mind.*

YOU DON'T HAVE TO BE A ROCKSTAR

One of the biggest challenges of academia is the comparison game. In some departments where students have to compete with one another for funding, it can be easy to understand how this may happen. Add to it a culture where one's accomplishments are water cooler, or rather coffee pot talk. In many departments there are weekly or monthly updates on student and faculty achievements. In association conventions and meetings, lifetime achievement awards are handed out. Awards for early career, mid-career, and everywhere in between. Everyone oohs and ahhs and congratulates themselves. It is rather funny when you think about it. And a little bit of a letdown. After any major accomplishment, usually we eventually return to baseline as we acclimate to whatever our new norm now includes. The sad part is how often we doubt ourselves, comparing ourselves to the standards which departments hold in great esteem. But the question becomes this: Do you plan to be a superstar, or can you be okay with where you are right now?

While the two are not mutually exclusive, often one must decide which is more important—the accolades or the timely completion of a degree? That said, I would not recommend applying for no grants, submitting zero papers for publication, and generally futzing around. The idea is that all good things come in moderation. Just like ice cream. Too much and you regret it and feel ill. Just the right amount and you are thoroughly satisfied. Believe it or not, the same applies to achievements while in graduate school. While I'm always impressed by my graduate students who land the major grants, publications and so forth, the question in my mental health practitioner mind is "yes, but at what price?"

There are those rare breeds of us that love every minute of research and graduate school. And I wouldn't say one has to be in this place to be successful (though of course it'd help significantly). But what I will say is that what you see isn't always what you get. And what your mom told you about "If it's too good to be true, it probably is" rings true. Everything comes at a price, and it is a matter of what you are willing to pay for it. Some may land amazing grants and top-tier journal publications but be miserable and unfulfilled in their personal lives. The same way that the partier is likely trying to drink away a week of poor lab performance and a future that seems to be going nowhere, the overachiever is rarely much better off internally. Again, I will say there are those super rare types who have everything going for them all the time. But I have yet to meet one in about 10 years of research. The reality is that something's got to give.

In my time in academia I have heard and seen it all. One lab I once visited featured a futon, complete with blanket and pillow. As I asked about its previous owner, the truth came out. It was a male graduate student who had been there for around 10 years. In case I haven't said it before, and even if I have, allow me to say it once more. THERE IS NO REASON WHY A PH.D. SHOULD TAKE 10 YEARS! Even if you get married, have children, get divorced, get married again, it still need not take that long.

There is a fine balance that is so hard to find in graduate school life. It is about how deeply does graduate school define your identity, and how much do you retain other parts of yourself? Graduate school is not the real world. Even though it may feel like it. Often people will settle in, which can be great. They buy houses, set down roots. But this can also be a very easy way to prolong graduate school as well. Add to it that extra data your advisor wants you to run, and pretty soon the end is nowhere in sight.

Your Turn!

★ *PhDeductions: Decrease the load and demand on yourself. Certainly there are major requirements and projects you must do for timely completion of your degree. But you don't have to say "yes" to every additional project or commitment thrown your way. While at the beginning of graduate school, your excitement can lead you to quickly fill up your plate as you maximize your experience, at some point you'll be juggling far more torches in the air than you'd like. Make a list of priorities. What are in tiers I, II, III, and IV? Get a sense of what is essential, what you'd like to do, and what can be put on the backburner.*

THE FINE ART OF FAKING IT

Cassandra, a Ph.D. student in English literature, sat in my office, tear-streaked face as she talked about a future unknown. She did not know when she would graduate, what her thesis project would be on, or even what she needed to do next. Feeling helpless and hopeless, she began to drift into depression. Her self-esteem suffered, she stayed up late at night on the computer, wasting away time and energy. She'd come into class the next day exhausted and unable to focus or concentrate. She wished someone would just tell her what to do.

One of the most well-kept secrets of academia is this— we all wing it ... almost all of the time. This is not to say that genius and careful planning are not the predecessors to some of the greatest innovations many fields have seen. But that said, a Ph.D. requires resourcefulness. If you can find out how to become an "expert" in something in one night and lecture on it the next day, faking it like a pro, then you should have little troubles. And the reality is that we do this often. In truth, the sheer volume of work required in many Ph.D. programs is in the realm of daunting. Many students become paralyzed by anxiety and fear that no way can they get everything done in time. Yes, your professors may require you to read 200 pages in the next week for one class, while another asks you to do a thorough literature review in a given topic. It is about setting limits and realizing that the work will always be there. It can stretch out and take days and nights if you really put 110% or even 100% into it.

By no means will I say, "actually, don't bother doing the work." But usually, students who are admitted into Ph.D. programs will typically have the wherewithal to do a pretty reasonable job at a task even if they put in 80%. Sometimes skimming, and using Google to fill in the blanks can save you time and frustration. The amount of times I entered a library for research purposes during my four years in graduate school can be counted on one hand (that would be missing a couple of fingers.) Spending hours scouring for that right book often is fruitless, and, in time, you come to learn what really is essential, and what is not.

Graduate students often complain to me in therapy that they have no clue how to do half of what their advisor wants them to do. Why do they do that? Yes, some advisors may be busy, distracted by other projects and so forth, but often they trust you. The process of becoming a professional means that one day you will stand up and draft studies, write brilliant papers, and make the rules. You will not always know everything about everything. Each new endeavor will force you to educate yourself on the norms and name of the game. The sooner you learn to edit your own abstracts and quickly turn them in without 10 revisions from your advisor, the sooner you can move onto the many projects you have. Yes, sometimes it is the advisor who sets up this precedent. But sometimes it can also be okay to learn through risking failure. Turn in that abstract with only 2 sets of revisions. See what happens. Often the extra eight will not have significantly altered the content of your submission anyway.

I learned this important lesson in trusting yourself and abilities early on in undergrad. I worked with a young female psychologist who I greatly admired. She was one of those women who seemed to have it all. Brains, beauty, charm, a great family life, and, of course, a very impressive body of academic research. I was in her office asking her about a project we would be doing together, when she opened her computer and just started typing it up right there on the spot. I remember I would have typically agonized before even starting, making sure I was using an adequate number of GRE-level words that would make me seem intellectual, but accessible. But no, instead this woman pretty much knocked out a draft of the entire proposal in about 15 minutes flat. I also remember one of my good friends in high school who got bumped up and put in my Calculus class. As I frantically flipped through my notes to figure out how to start the homework assignment, my friend would sit there smacking her gum and twirling her hair around her finger as she accurately and quickly solved derivative problem sets. The lesson: it's all about mindset. Take a deep breath and let it happen.

Those who enter top schools and Ph.D. programs do not have superhuman IQs. I know this for a fact—as part of my educational training as a psychologist, I have administered at least a dozen IQ tests to friends, top students, and others. Most are around average or a bit higher, but no Einsteins in the group (not that Einstein would have necessarily aced our standard battery of tests given their cultural biases). The point is things become as difficult as we make them. We are the ones that determine through our thought processes that things are stressful, hard, etc. Perspective allows us to overcome these mental biases.

As such, trust yourself. Trust that you are on the process of being an emerging professional. One day you will make the rules. You will not have an advisor to tell you what to do every step of the way. The sooner you can learn to be independent, the better. Professionally, your options will grow exponentially as well. You will not be tied to one person, type of job, or institution. In business, they often refer to it as diversification. A good investment portfolio is one marked by diverse interests. It is the same for academics.

As a result of your program, you will likely be asked to stretch yourself anyway. Teach a class you've never taught, even if you have no teaching experience. Learn to use and operate a state-of-the-art machine that costs over a million dollars as breakable and fragile as it may seem (and scary). Instead of shying away from these often uncomfortable experiences, learn to embrace them. Sure, you may not be the best lecturer. Maybe you learned that you do better with one-on-one advising. Either way, you will conquer your insecurities and may learn something new about yourself. Earlier in the book, I talked about the problem with putting all of your eggs in one basket. The same goes professionally. By sticking with what is easy and safe, you run into trouble if, at some point, you become disillusioned by the prospect of entering a Research I institution or whatever other route you had planned out.

Your Turn!

★ *PhDiversify: While the goal is not to overload yourself during graduate school, you also don't want to feel stuck or pigeon-holed in one area. When all of your energy goes into one direction, you can start to feel bored, or a lack of challenge. Sometimes it is at this point that students start to procrastinate. However, by staying on top of your work and selecting maybe one or two other activities, projects, depart-mental service committees, you might see other ways you can contrib-ute academically other than just one program of research. Finally, remember that you don't have to be an expert! You are a student and learning. Many are just pretending until they get things right, so don't be afraid not to be at the top of the class in a new venture.*

A WORD ON IMPOSTER SYNDROME

If you've been carefully reading and applying many of the ideas posited in this book thus far, imposter syndrome may have been less likely to be an issue for you. However, among graduate student women, this can be a very common phenomenon. To further elu-cidate this concept, imposter syndrome is a term coined by clini-cal psychologists Pauline Clance and Suzanne Imes in 1978. They found that many high-achieving women feel like a fraud. Instead of attributing their successes to internal abilities, they consider fac-tors such as timing, luck, likeability, or even physical attractiveness as leading to their achievements. As such they are plagued by a nagging feeling that perhaps they don't belong in graduate school, that one day someone will "find them out."

Imposter syndrome is very real and a common presenting concern at university counseling centers. Many times women of color, first generation, and low-income women may be at high-er risk for developing such feelings. Research has shown that upbringing and even birth order can lead to a propensity toward developing an imposter syndrome orientation. For example, if you were the youngest child of a family with a high-achieving old-er sibling, you may have made your mark in the family as the cute, funny one, rather than the brains of the family. As a result, despite years of success and achievement, one may be less readily likely to accept their excellence as their own.

An important factor in decreasing feelings of being an impos-ter comes from a multi-pronged approach. On the one hand, reaching out to women as discussed in previous sections, is an excellent means of finding validation and support. On the other hand, professional treatment such as counseling can be a deeply rewarding means of discussing the history and manifestation of this occurrence in one's life. The first time I ever even heard of imposter syndrome wasn't until after my Ph.D. program, when I was on clinical internship. It was at a presentation and despite having always considered myself to be a confident person, many of its features hit home. It was an "aha" moment of sorts, and just being aware of such a phenomena made me more mindful of moments when I was likely to fall into discounting my achievements.

Your Turn!

★ *PhDoubts: Having doubts about your ability to succeed can be perfectly natural. It can also be common for many high-achieving women to have difficulty taking full credit of their many incredible accomplishments. They live in constant denial of how truly amazing they are. Put aside those doubts and take a moment to practice savoring your accomplishments and truly congratulating yourself. Take ownership of your successes. During graduate school my friends and I used to joke that we needed "insta-confetti" to mark each other's accomplishments as they so often went unacknowledged. So don't be afraid to celebrate your abstract being accepted for a conference or just passing that tough statistics class. Douse yourself in imaginary confetti and perhaps treat yourself to a nice meal or movie night. Remember, you do deserve it! It takes practice to internalize it*

CHAPTER 6

CREATING A HALF-LIFE

"A woman is like a tea bag: you cannot tell how strong she is until you put her in hot water."

—*Nancy Reagan*

SELF-PRESERVATION

In my experience, often one of the biggest struggles many graduate students face is overcoming the bureaucracies and politics of their department. Everything from whether or not you pass a proposal or defense to whether or not you will be awarded summer funding depends upon your ability to negotiate the politics of graduate school. That said, this isn't a season of the television show "Survivor" either. Alliances are important, but they also aren't everything. I have heard graduate students complain about which professors have adversarial relationships and how that will simply ruin everything. On the contrary, while there could be some influences, these claims are often over-exaggerated. If it were a dictatorship or totalitarian regime, graduate schools would have been shut down ages ago. After all, if any one knows anything about graduate school, it is that is the furthest thing from a money making endeavor. The economists could have readily packed up their things and headed to MBA programs, the chemists and biologists to medical schools instead and so on. So don't believe the hype. I spoke with a young woman once who had quite literally worked herself up into a tizzy over this alliance battleground.

Negotiating politics is tricky business. No one said it was easy. But allowing it to run your life can quickly become the fastest energy drain around. Like I've said many times before, getting a Ph.D. successfully is less about the work to be done, but rather mastering the dramas. It is important then to begin understanding how to create balance. For example, I was regularly given static from fellow students for my physical absence from lab. Frankly, it just didn't make any sense to me. Why should I sit in a confined space far from my refrigerator and bathroom and come in to lab when I had no subjects to run or other things that explicitly required me to be in a laboratory? Granted, one caveat I must note is that my advisor allowed me the autonomy to make this decision and trusted I was doing fine so long as work was being accomplished in a timely manner. As such this was another major factor I attribute to decreasing the drama quotient in my academic life.

Labs can be wonderful. They can allow for collaborations, exchange of ideas, and an overall collegial atmosphere. That, however, is in a perfect world. One where your fellow graduate students are not under the pressure of grading 150 exams by the next day, where another graduate student isn't going through a horrible breakup, and where a third one isn't trying to one-up you every other minute. But as we know, we rarely live in this idyllic academic setting. Unfortunately, it becomes about self-preservation. How do you protect number one? Yes, this sounds selfish. And as women, we are most of all expected to care about our fellow woman and others around us. We are often the nurturers, the mediators, and go to all lengths to comfort one another. This is wonderful in times of grave tragedies and major life mishaps. Yet graduate school can be a hotbed of mishaps. Every day someone will have a dilemma. Guaranteed.

There are larger forces at play that may explain this. For example, an external locus of control can be one such factor. Psychological studies have shown that when elders in residential living facilities were given control over small details such as decorating their rooms and arranging furniture as they wished, they had better outcomes. Meaning they lived longer. This is an extreme example, but illustrates just how important a sense of control can be. For graduate students, there is often a sense that they have absolutely no control. One minute their advisor loves them, the next they are piling on loads of extra work. Studies to run, papers to read, classes to T.A. or teach. They live in such a manner for four or more years. After awhile, this can start to take a toll. We would laugh that some of us engaged in escapist behaviors. I recall a particular summer where I was particularly concerned about the nature of Edward and Bella's relationship in the teen vampire saga, *Twilight*. So much so that I wound up publishing a research article on the series. But for that summer, if Bella was curled up in a ball in the middle of the forest, I was right there with her. It was certainly a better place to be at times than graduate school.

It is at these times that many unhealthy behaviors may begin. Some graduate students fall into a category about which we often joked—the lifelong student…the wannabe undergrad. I've definitely known my fair share of graduate students who had two homes: lab and the local bar or pub. Though it was unkind, many of us negatively viewed those who had been in our department for four to five years without so much as a Master's degree to show for their time. Their issue, we determined, was an overage of weekend partying and lack of dedication to their research. One might be able to rationalize this as not that big of a deal. They will eventually move on, and all that will be left are fond memories of the good old days. This would be fine, except as a clinical psychologist I can tell you many of these students engaged in what would clinically be defined as alcohol abuse, while others were teetering on the edge of alcohol dependence, or what we colloquially refer to as alcoholism.

The stereotype around alcohol issues is commonplace—an individual who drinks all day everyday. But according to diagnostic criteria, the situation is more complex. Things like tolerance (which so many boast about) and binge drinking can be much more serious indicators than are recognized. Many believe college is the time for drinking, even a little bit to excess. But statistics show 1 in 3 college students have a diagnosable problem with alcohol. This is no laughing matter.

All this said, what's a girl to do? It really does become a delicate balance of engaging and disengaging. One of my biggest gripes about graduate school was the overage of complaining going on. The meta-message was that there was always something that was not okay, and that we were ultimately doomed. I like to consider myself an optimist by nature. A bubbly type many would say. And this drove me mad. The victimized poor helpless graduate student was the costume fellow graduate student expected me to put on, but one which I refused to wear.

Looking for an easy way to explain the importance of self-care to my clients, I came up with an empirically-supported model I call E.M.P.O.W.E.R. Originally published in my column for *Psychology Today*, below is the explication of the science behind the model. For the purposes of this book, I have also created a supplemental chart which can be used to take the theoretical and apply it practically in your everyday life.

Exercise. Exercise, nutrition, and sleep are three major elements of physical health that have a direct relationship to your emotional and mental well-being. Many feel that exercise means a hefty time commitment, or imagine significant intensity. Age, medical conditions, mobility, and other factors certainly may impede the amount and duration of exercise in which one may be able to engage. But the bottom line is movement. It can be a short walk during lunchtime, or taking the stairs instead of the elevator as you hustle and bustle around the department or lab. While initially it may be tiresome if unaccustomed, small steps can make a huge difference!

Psychological research is increasingly realizing the important link between exercise and mood. According to research by Dr. James Blumenthal of Duke University, epidemiological data suggests that active individuals tend to be less depressed than inactive individuals. Further, his study with colleagues (2007) indicates the effect of exercise to be comparable to that of antidepressant medication for the treatment of major depressive disorder. In the follow-up to this experimental study, they found that those who continued to exercise experienced less depressive symptoms, indicating that exercise may be instrumental in preventing relapse as well.

The role of sleep and nutrition should not be ignored either. Poor sleep, lack of sleep, and sleep disturbance can lead to irritability, tension, and even depressive symptoms. Getting one's sleep back on track is extremely important, and can improve wellness in a myriad of areas. Sleep is also related to key functions such as memory consolidation as well as immune functioning. It helps improve your odds of not getting sick when all the undergrads in your class are coughing on you or when your lab mates are dropping like flies during flu and cold season.

We've been taught about nutrition since our elementary school days. The image of the dietary guideline pyramid is one that remains emblazoned in my memory. However, the guidelines have changed, and there is still debate on how accurate the current recommendations are. Yet, some staples remain the same. Including fruits, vegetables, and adequate hydration are important, as is avoiding excess sugars, fats, and alcohol. The effects of a sugar crash or hangover often manifest not only physically, but also emotionally. It is commonsensical that when we are putting good fuel into our system, our bodily engines run cleaner as well.

Meditate. Research is increasingly showing the health benefits of meditation for a range of physical and mental concerns. While practiced regularly in many Eastern traditions long before its introduction into Western medicine, its effects are substantial. There are many forms of meditation, ranging from Zen meditation to mindfulness-based stress reduction meditation programs. Though many associate meditation as a form of stress reduction, meditation in its purest form has no goals. It is awareness for the sake of awareness. It is a form of quieting the mind, in a world where our attention is so often divided. Prayer is functionally quite similar to meditation, and most major religious practices have a meditative component. For example, praying the rosary may be considered meditative for some.

Positivity. Positive psychology involves working from a strengths-based model, as opposed to a deficits-based one. Instead of focusing on identifying pathology, the intent is to increase overall wellness through a variety of means. For example, there is the idea of an "attitude of gratitude" which may involve keeping a gratitude journal and is referenced in this book. The simple act of writing down one or two things daily that one is grateful for can increase one's happiness over time.

Among the many topics positive psychology researchers are examining, one is the construct of resilience. Recent research by Dr. Mark Seery of the University at Buffalo SUNY, indicates a potential silver lining to experiencing negative life events. He explains that according to past research, it was assumed that no negative life events were optimal. However, his research indicates that some lifetime adversity predicts better outcomes than high adversity or no adversity at all. Essentially, it suggests the possible benefits of adversity. How's that for glass half-full?

Outdoors. One of the most accessible but often overlooked means of improving mood involves getting into the great outdoors. Many of the nation's largest metropolitan areas are increasingly understanding this concept, as urban planners and architects discuss the infusion of "green spaces" into their designs. While not everyone may be able to run to their nearest white sand beach, other elements such as rivers, creeks, mountains, and beautiful snowcapped fields can invoke a sense of inner peace. Taking the time to marvel at nature's beauty, wherever you are in the country can be truly awe-inspiring. From leaves and ladybugs, to dew on blades of grass, the closer you look, the more miracles you may uncover. Most college campuses are a huge win in this arena. Many have gorgeous sprawling lawns or are at the very least close to mountains, lakes, or beaches. Take advantage of that and get into the great outdoors!

Work. Though potentially confounding at first as to why work would be on the list, its inclusion refers to engaging and meaningful work. Csikszentmihalyi's pioneering studies on flow theory explains that when engaged in work that blends the right amount of challenge and skill, we are fully immersed in it. It is in such states that we are unaware of the passing of time. Creative energies may increase, and it can be similar to "the zone" that many athletes experience. While it may be ideal to be able to experience flow in our jobs, this may not always be the case. Yet flow can also be achieved when engaging in hobbies such as playing a musical instrument, gardening, cooking, reading, or writing.

Further, research suggests that among those who live the longest are those who work the hardest. Research outlined in the new book, The Longevity Project, makes fascinating conclusions.

Co-author Dr. Howard Friedman said in an interview with The Monitor, "People are being given rotten advice to slow down, take it easy, stop worrying, and retire to Florida. The Longevity Project discovered that those who worked the hardest lived the longest. The responsible and successful achievers thrived in every way, especially if they were dedicated to things and people beyond themselves."

Enlighten. Dr. Friedman's words about dedicating oneself to causes beyond themselves is in line with the notion of enlightenment. We may have varying understandings and impressions of what enlightenment encompasses. The reality is that it need not be something mystical or otherworldly. I see it as being about self-actualization and improvement. It can involve educating the mind about astronomy, anthropology, geography, or linguistics. It may involve stepping outside your door to help those in need. Whether it is random acts of kindness, or a concerted effort to improve yourself through education, the idea is expansion. Expanding our connectedness to other ideas, people, and worlds. Enlightenment is a broad concept, and can mean different things to different people. Think for a moment what it means to you. How can you integrate it into your own life?

Relationships. Relationships can take many forms. Family, friends, partners, spouses, co-workers, and even pets can provide us with empathy, support, and a community network. Relationships can be one of the first things to go when bogged down by daily stressors. Who has time for a leisurely coffee date with a friend when there are a dozen items on the day's to-do list? However, the concept of "social support buffering" is essentially a superstar in psychological research. It could have the psychological equivalent of its own star on the Hollywood Walk of Fame. It is used to explain coping and resilience in the face of a plethora of stressors and adversities that we may face. Whether it is divorce, racism, unemployment, or a natural disaster, individuals typically desire social support to mitigate adverse effects. Even positive psychologists have made a nod to social relationships as being a component to happiness and overall well-being.

I share the preceding model of empowerment as I believe it can remind us of living our best lives. The one that is here right now. Not when we weigh 10 pounds less, or when our income is higher, we meet Mr. Right, or finish our Ph.D. It encourages us to take leaps of faith, and have support whatever the outcome. We can go outside for a run, but meditate in solitude as well. One of my favorite quotes comes from the dancer Agnes de Mille. She said, "Living is a form of not being sure, not knowing what next or how…We guess. We may be wrong, but we take leap after leap in the dark."

Who knows precisely what the next hour will bring? Even if we get it right, affective forecasting research tells us that our predictions about our reactions to it may be very wrong. In Appendix B you will find my corresponding E.M.P.O.W.E.R. checklist for easy reference. It will challenge you to create and meet goals related to your overall well-being.

Your Turn!

★ *PhDazzle: A well-balanced life is the key to thriving versus surviving. Try out the E.M.P.O.W.E.R. checklist for a week. Get in touch with your inner self—reflect, meditate, and exercise to a power soundtrack. Do something you know is good for you but that you too often feel guilty about doing. Your mind, body, and spirit will thank you!*

THE MOST IMPORTANT CARE IS SELF-CARE

My first year of graduate school I was on the phone with one of my best friends discussing how completely frazzled I felt. I marveled at how she managed to keep her hair cut, highlighted and so well-maintained. Her nails were impeccable and she basically looked like the real life version of graduate school Barbie all while excelling in her program. "How do you do it?!" I asked. She told me one of the key secrets she learned early on—one that was even difficult for her to internalize. Self-care is the most important care. Until you can take care of yourself, you can't take care of others. In mental health, this is particularly salient. But for other fields, this still applies.

If you are unable to do what is needed to stay feeling healthy, fresh, rested, and relaxed (as much as one can be in graduate school), it will be harder to give to others. As we know about graduate school, it is all about the giving—extra time to train those lab undergrads, to meet with students during office hours to discuss their papers and how they were graded, to serve as an ad-hoc reviewer, and so on. As women, we are socialized to be givers. We aim to please, because we were taught this is what good little girls do. It becomes part of our identity. Over time, if we don't give back to ourselves, it can start to take a toll. And frankly, it starts to show.

While I hesitate to make explicit recommendations as to how one defines "upkeep," I do think it is important to value and integrate this into one's regular life. If you wait for the day when you have time, that day will never come. In Appendix C you will find a list of free apps that help may help serve as a reminder of goals you set for self-care. Additionally, they can help you track your mood, areas of growth, and assist in keeping you balanced as you make your way through graduate school and life.

Your Turn!

★ *PhDapper: There is nothing wrong with taking care of yourself inside and out. You may think that being a graduate student means your needs go to the bottom of the list, but that's not true! Below try the "spa day at home" activity. Add, modify, and do as much or as little as you'd like. Play around with it—you might just have fun and feel rested afterwards.*

Spa Day at Home

Many times when it comes to the notion of taking a day to relax, students bemoan the fact that they can't afford a massage or day at the spa. Even if that is exactly what they need. But savvy graduate students can find short-cuts. Here are a few ideas to get the creative juices flowing:

Morning

Wake up when you desire. Yes, sleep in. Many students feel the burden of starting at the crack of dawn and drag throughout the day, attempting to use coffee to make up for sleep. So start your day off right, and well rested. Nap later in the day if needed, because after all, we are getting you rejuvenated, and that might involve making up for lost hours of sleep. Then begin with some healthy stretching, yoga, breathing, meditation or prayer. If there is a yoga studio you've been meaning to go to but never have, today is the day to jump in and do it. Or, just put in that DVD, or watch something on YouTube to get you inspired. Then, have a yummy breakfast you typically wouldn't have. My favorites are homemade chocolate chip pancakes with fresh sliced strawberries or vanilla cinnamon French toast using healthy bread and a hefty side of mixed berries.

Mid-Morning/Noon

Decide what type of tone you'd like to set for the day. Tropical get-away? Buy some refreshing pineapple juice and sip while you read a magazine or book for fun. Purchase a bottle of brightly colored nail polish to coordinate with your theme. Looking for a more relaxing retreat? Light a vanilla or lavender-scented candle and put on soothing music. Maybe some jasmine green tea, mint, or chamomile tea will add to the experience.

Also, think about what needs you've been neglecting. Fried hair? Try an at-home deep conditioning treatment. One easy trick I learned was to soak your hair in olive oil and put it in a shower cap. Leave it on for about 20-30 minutes, get in to the shower and start soaping up, and doing your regular routine. Let the steam further activate the oils, and rinse out last. Though a little messy (oily, naturally) you'd be amazed by how soft and shiny it leaves hair. You can experiment with other oils such as coconut if desired.

If your skin needs some TLC, get yourself a nicely scented body lotion or moisturizer. I found myself drawn to energizing and natural citrus-scented lotion that was both soothing to my skin and senses. Also, have fun with natural facials. I found an easy recipe for a honey mask that I started making while in graduate school. Honey can add a bit of a glow to the skin. Add a dash of cinnamon for an anti-bacterial effect. Salt or sugar can act as an exfoliant, while adding lemon juice can help with skin discoloration. I usually would eye ball the amounts, adding enough dry ingredients to make it a paste. Otherwise, honey drips down your face and it's a sticky mess all over. That said, it always helps to apply, lay down and relax for a while until you wash it off. It can also help to do this prior to a shower in case it does drip.

Much like in the morning, eat well. Too often stressed students under-fuel or fuel with unhealthy ingredients.

Think of the perfect spa meal—for me that involves a delicious salad with chicken, dried cranberries, fresh berries, walnuts, feta, and a balsamic vinaigrette. This doesn't mean you should deprive yourself either. Usually my healthy meal is accompanied by an appropriate portion of a lavender gelato, mango sorbet, or coffee ice cream.

Evening/Night

Provide yourself with internal nourishment. Write down your thoughts in a journal, call a good friend, have a Skype date with a soul sister. A dose of laughter is also some of the best medicine. Watch a new comedy or an old favorite. Perhaps even a film that inspires. End the day the same way you started it. Meditate, pray, stretch. Go to bed at a timely hour and notice the difference on your mood the next day.

Prioritize having a "spa day" to yourself at least monthly. You might find this day actually involves basic hygiene needs such as going to the dentist or getting a hair cut or trim. It might mean getting your pants hemmed or dry cleaning dropped off. You might have to go to the grocery store before you can even make that yummy breakfast, lunch, and dinner for your luxurious day. Or your day might even involve a trip to the convenience store where you'll sample moisturizers, peruse magazines, and buy a few inexpensive items that boost your mood. While you can't buy happiness, you can pick up a few items that can help you feel better.

Also, remember that the idea of this day is by no means a superficial attempt at embracing the stereotypical "female" role of prettying yourself up or being ultra feminine. The idea is doing something for yourself that maybe you've wanted to do, but have kept putting off. So this day will look different for various individuals. Just don't be afraid to try it. Students who I've "assigned" this task to in therapy often come back amazed how much better they feel. Sometimes all they did was get a hair-cut and hit the gym. But it made an impact nonetheless. What effect will it have on you? Only you can try it out and see…

CRASHING THE MBA PROM

During graduate school, I was surrounded by MBA students. Okay, this might be an exaggeration, but it's not entirely far from the truth. This was a product of living in graduate housing where roughly 50% of our residents were either law or business students. As a result, most of my neighbors were made up of this demographic. As many of them also happened to be quite gregarious, I came to learn about nuances of their academic programs, social activities, and general way of life. In this time I also learned one shocking fact about our law and business students. While the law students had a "barrister's ball," the MBAs had, wait for it….a prom! As one who never made it to my own homecoming or prom dances, I became determined to make it to the prom, even if it wasn't my own. In retrospect, I don't know what was wrong with me. But part of the fun side of graduate school involves the social antics and adventures one has. So while remaining focused, motivated and passionate about one's field paves the way to success, so does a healthy social life and a little bit of fun.

Though motivating graduate students to engage in social activities can feel like pulling teeth at times, don't be afraid to be the ring-leader. Look at your surroundings and determine what your options are. In the Midwest we had fun with corn mazes, apple picking in Michigan, going up to the lake, and cultural events in Chicago. Friends held Fourth of July barbeques, Halloween costume parties, Secret Santas, Valentine's Day singles celebrations, girls-only movie nights, and even a soup coOKing dinner club. There are many ways to get creative without falling into the rut of gathering at someone's house with some alcohol.

Also, feel free to embrace the ways of other crowds. During graduate school I wound up befriending our creative writing students and joined along for open mic nights and all sorts of musical events. And although I was disappointed I didn't get to attend the fancy Kentucky Derby event our MBAs put on, their "go big or go home" social ways definitely gave me some ideas of ways of thinking outside the typical social box.

While typically the social structure of one's graduate school experience is pre-determined by factors such as geography, there can be quite a bit of flexibility and opportunity to shape one's experience. For example, a graduate student in Manhattan may have something different to do every day of the week. And yet, for some, such large cities can actually feel isolating and individuals are scattered all over town. A mid-sized school in a rural area may not be your cup of tea either, but weekly football games and tailgates may get you out of the house. Or perhaps, you will find something in the middle—access to the big city if you'd like it, but something quieter if you need that too. Explore around and find your "regular" activities. By the end of my graduate school experience I had $2 burger Tuesday nights, $1 Wednesday movie night, Thursday Irish pub night (often including delicious chocolate cake) followed by an open mic at another venue. Then the Friday football parade in the afternoon kicked off the weekend. If I was very ambitious, there was a midnight Thursday drummer's circle to attend as well.

In truth, I'm actually not much of a social butterfly. But the facetious joke of the four-day MBA weekend spanning from Thursday to Sunday was a bit of an inspiration. How did they manage to get a degree, a lucrative job and still have fun, I wondered. Just because my program was double in length with some more hoops to jump through didn't mean I couldn't experience something similar. In fact, in some ways I felt I deserved it even more because of the time I was investing. Although graduate school can feel clique-ish at times, this is no reason to deprive yourself of experiencing connections with students from all disciplines and walks of life. Too often I've heard from students, "But there is no one to hang out with." Trust me, they are there. You just have to find them. Many times my own colleagues were too busy with lab or other projects and rightfully so—they had demanding advisors and schedules. But I wasn't going to miss out on opportunities because I had no one to do them with. MBA prom? Why not? Sign me up.

Your Turn!

★ *PhDaze: Stuck in a daze sometimes after hours of readings, running test subjects or writing? Get out of the lab! Find an activity, a partner to do it with, or just fly solo in the ways of the true independent women. Don't let yourself get bogged down in work all day everyday. Breaking out of wherever your workspace is can clear your mind and provide better ideas and energy to execute them. Learn from whoever your school's most social students are. How do they balance a work life and personal life? Try out an activity you've been hearing about but never actually tried. Maybe it is square dancing lessons in the community center or a movie on the quad. Get out, explore, and have a little bit of fun.*

Part III

Polishing: Graduate School
(Years 4-6: Yes, I stopped at 6)

CHAPTER 7

DON'T GET PHED UP

"You must do that which you think you cannot do."
—*Eleanor Roosevelt*

WHY SO MUCH NEGATIVITY?

I recall one break during graduate school when I flew back home. I was somewhere in the middle of my program and I remember my parents providing me with some very valuable feedback. They suddenly turned to me and asked, "What is with all of the complaining? Since you've gotten home, that's all you've done." I was shocked as I hadn't even realized this. Was it that I was irritable or really just finding something negative to say about every scenario? The people I look up to most have always been those who are high energy and positive. As such, that is what I have aimed to emulate throughout my life. But somehow I'd turned into the Grinch that stole graduate school. Unprepared to respond to this, I thought long and hard about how I'd come across as out of line. And how hadn't it even occurred to me that I was a giant complainer?

In his book *The Squeaky Wheel*, Dr. Guy Winch writes about the cultural phenomenon of excessive complaining in our society. We complain about everything he explains and are ineffective in getting what we want. However, there is something unique to graduate school in that everything is fair game to complain about. Although seemingly upbeat, in grad school I briefly had a roommate who was, shall we say, prone to complaint. Despite moments of incredible cheer, she always was upset about something. This constant negative energy infiltrated my daily living environment.

I came to observe that friends, classmates, nearly everyone in the graduate school bubble had a beef with something. All of the time. Stipends too low, poor housing options, failing research, boring course requirements to fulfill, too many papers to grade, not enough subjects in their studies, advisor's lack of appreciation, no attractive people to date, no sane people to date, don't get me started on the fact that "everybody" is married, on and on...

Ironically, in graduate school, the culture of complaining is reinforced. This is the stuff of bonding. No one gets credit for sharing their triumphs and joys. No, people prefer to show their battle scars. It becomes the sob story Olympics. Who was worst off this week in the department? During my tenure at Notre Dame, a bright upbeat young female researcher came as a visiting international scholar from the Netherlands. She was one of the individuals in graduate school from whom I learned a couple invaluable life lessons. One day while discussing my attempts to stop working on weekends she shared her surprising observations of the "American way." She shared her experience that students wear excess work like a badge of honor. Evenings, weekends, they work and they are proud to claim this as a sign of being better, working harder than others. In the Netherlands, she explained work still got done, but not at the expense of individuals' personal lives. They took the train to visit friends on weekends, spent evenings gathered together over dinner. None of this microwave meal in front of the television with journal articles littered all over a worn couch scenario so common among U.S. graduate students.

The question is, who changes this culture? Do you feed into it and slowly find yourself becoming increasingly miserable as you are surrounded by disgruntled colleagues? In some ways, by not connecting with this culture, you also run the risk of not being fully integrated into the normative culture of the department. So do you feign misery at the departmental holiday party and then sneak off and rejoice secretly at how well life is really going back in the privacy of your own home?

The trick to overcoming a toxic culture is by establishing healthier groups outside of the department. This not only leads to more balance but can also provide a healthier perspective. In befriending many students in professional and master's degree programs, I came to see how privileged I really was to be pursuing a doctorate degree free of charge while still young and energized. I saw that I was more than halfway through the program and that it'd be over in no time. Often these students only had one to three years on campus while I had more time to soak in a once in a lifetime opportunity, whether it meant going to coveted football games, experiencing winter wonderland snowy conditions, or access to Chicago. I realized that instead of wishing away a period of my life, this actually had the potential to be one of the best periods of my life.

One might wonder how one accesses and establishes these groups outside of one's department. You'd be surprised, but most graduate students are craving the same thing. Engineers are tired of hanging out with other engineers and business students can't stand to talk about that ethics assignment with one more colleague or be forced to "schmooze." So go to those awkward grad student socials with the expectation that you are strong enough to overcome the initial uneasiness. Also, look into the community. Are there dance or yoga studios? Perhaps there are young professional associations. Apartment communities, off campus, gyms, wine and canvas nights, the options are endless. It's a matter of changing your perspective. Throughout life I've made friends anywhere from on the bus to an airplane, while checking the mail to taking out the trash. It doesn't take any unique skill. Just a desire to connect with individuals who strike you as possessing the type of energy you'd like to surround yourself with.

Finally, it is important to notice the impact of this culture on your own life. You might have read this entire section and thought, "So what? Grad students are negative, big deal, move on." The reality is these subtle factors do impact your progress as they influence motivation. When you view your life as going poorly, you may feel that you have less of a direct impact on your successful degree completion. Instead of looking for innovative solutions to help with that low participant pool problem, you will just complain about it and hope it works itself out. So be careful and monitor those thoughts. Going down a negative road? Maybe it's time for some self-care. Go back to Part II and try the Spa Day at Home or tap into those coping strategies you listed earlier.

Your Turn!

★ *PhDiscard: Ditch those negative thoughts and complaining ways. Make a list of all the things "going wrong" in your life. Now take an objective look at it. Are there ways you can find solutions or change your perspective? For example, if you are unhappy with your dating life, are you actually putting yourself in situations to meet and mingle or are you just staying home every Friday and Saturday night complaining about it? Do you hate where you live? Look at your budget. Can you afford to move or get a roommate to upgrade to a nicer residence? Do you feel like your advisor hates you? As scary as it sounds you might be able to have a candid conversation with them or at least get positive support and validation from older students in the program. Remember the old adage—there are no problems, only solutions waiting to be discovered.*

I GUARANTEE YOU, THERE WILL BE HATERS

When one embarks upon a journey with hope and optimism, there will be often be those who insist on pointing out the clouds in the sky and convince you that a storm is brewing. Too often individuals seem to be waiting for the downfall of others, if for no other reason than to feel better about themselves. Consequently, the energetic, hopeful, joyous, and kind sometimes are the perfect targets that get trampled upon or criticized. Even if one doesn't fit into this category, the tendency for graduate school to pick one apart is ubiquitous. I've heard everything from one's facial expressions to vocal inflections criticized by faculty in graduate programs across the country. This seems to be the norm more so than the exception. Unfortunately, this can serve as a green light for such behaviors to be emulated by graduate students and passed down to future generations.

Critics will prey on the unique individuals who don't fit the standard mold. I remember one time first year when I ebulliently burst into my new cohort mate's lab to chitchat. This was about a month into the program. A male from her lab turned to me and asked if I was her friend as he'd never met me before. "Actually, um, I'm one of the new graduate students," I replied feeling a little out of place. Obviously something about me did not scream "grad student." Maybe it was my nearly giddy excitement rare in a department, or my Southern California valley accent from childhood that every so often slips up into my speech. Whatever it was, it was the beginning of the messages I faced that implied, " You do not belong here." I should qualify this statement and say it was by no means everyone. It was rather symptomatic of a larger culture and system.

Academia inherently has a rather arrogant and strict description of what is "professional" and "unprofessional." What is "appropriate" and "inappropriate." You either fit this prototype or are an outcast of sorts. I was fortunate to have a highly supportive advisor who would come to bat for me. There were professors who understood what I was trying to do. I wanted to break stereotypes of the common academic. I wanted to be relatable, make graduate study accessible to more people. I aimed to discard the elite factor and speak a common language informed by high caliber research. I came into the program with one of the lengthiest publication records among my colleagues, but I didn't announce it at every opportunity as many do (wait, I think I'm doing it right now, but hopefully you see my point). I didn't care about being that graduate student who everyone praises due to productivity. As such I was sometimes treated as though I was at the very bottom of the proverbial food chain. It wasn't necessarily anything that anyone said. These things are rarely ever so explicit. It was something far more subtle. The fact that saying "hello" to faculty you don't know can seem too bold. Or feeling that every time you raised your hand to defend the opposite side of an argument, you had to come in with the gusto of a trial lawyer.

As women, we may be prone to taking these things personally. I'm often amazed to see the difference in how males in academia often treat or interpret these very same criticisms. Yes, it is definitely stereotypical to say women "get emotional." But I will openly say that I do. I have feelings and they get hurt. That is possibly one of the greatest challenges of academia. However, developing resiliency and thicker skin might help.

I was once told early on by a professor in my undergraduate honors program that the best thing to do early on was to never take writing critique personally. The sooner you emotionally detach, the quicker you could advance, and the better your work would be. It was easy to ascribe that mentality to writing. But it is harder when it is about ideas. Because ideas are personal. And the way they can be shot down in public forums can often be nothing short of humiliating.

FACT: research can show almost anything. Few things are un-debatable facts in any field. Most are theories and plausible findings that indicate, suggest, and imply. Very rarely do they ever prove conclusively. This is both a blessing in disguise as well as a curse. You will rarely ever be flat out wrong. But there will be times when faculty and students will try to play that game. You know, the one that has no winner—the one that is useless and does little else than irritate you. My research is better than your research. My theory is more well-supported than yours because the methodology was more sophisticated than the ones you are referencing, and so on and so forth. Depending on how far you will take it, it eventually will become personal. Well, the author of this paper is from Yale. The author of the study you based your dissertation off of is from Montana State University. But low and behold even if you wind up at Yale, there will still be a reason why you are not good enough. So don't even bother playing that game in the first place. People will critique. Sometimes these critiques will be constructive and useful. Other times, you can throw them out the window. But don't let your self-esteem or worth get lost in the shuffle.

The picturesque academic is easy to imagine. White male, standard American name, with just the right amount of grey streaks in his hair to appear distinguished. Am I suggesting that women, and particularly women of color have no hope? Of course not. In many ways though, we will have to work harder, and it becomes taxing. It also explains why women of color have the highest attrition rate of all graduate student populations. There are many more barriers they may face. Some might be the first to attend higher institutes of learning, or be of lower SES. They may hold the very intersecting identities that academia needs to increase its diversity.

During my training, I came to meet a very inspirational and visionary woman who I am proud to call a friend. Though she first stood out to me as the sweet woman with a welcoming smile and adorable hearing dog, I came to learn she held an identity influenced by many factors. She was White but also Jewish. She identified as lesbian, and read lips like no other, teaching our training cohort the nice and naughty sign language words. She worked to understand therapy client issues from the many spectacular lenses she was afforded due to her lived experience with kindness and compassion unlike anything I'd seen before. I share her example as a woman who understood power and privilege from multiple stances. It is one thing to be discriminated against as a woman, but it's another when you don't have basic access to educational videos because they don't include closed captioning. Or if you are seen as White and a member of the privileged group only to be judged for your sexual orientation or religious background. These are matters worth considering and as minorities we are all in it together. It is not about "my struggle is worse than your struggle." Rather they are different and unique, and require sensitivity and mutual support.

When you are able to recognize and then ignore the many injustices around you, it allows you to remember why you came here in the first place…why you've made it to graduate school. If you've already overcome so many barriers to getting in which is the hardest part, why let the culture or other external factors affect you so greatly? It is a hard point to remember, but one that must be retained. Once you are able to learn to take things in stride, it helps prepare you for the inevitable tiffs along the way.

Your Turn!

★ *PhDiversity: Graduate schools often seem to be promoting one giant oxymoron. While they come up with mission statements attesting to importance and value of diversity, their actions don't often back up their words. Through subtle policies, criticisms, and actions they send the message that the diverse applicants they are admitting*

*need to conform to a pre-determined mold. So don't feel ashamed or
that you need to drastically change yourself to fit in. Remember that
you are needed just as you are in your field. Little girls receive their
inspiration from the women that dared to stand apart. The women
that blazed paths where there were none before. So remember that no
matter how out of place you may feel at times, you matter, an incredible amount. Think about volunteering with underserved groups or
in a capacity where you can be a mentor to younger populations. For
example, Girls, Inc., is a non-profit with programming for young girls
across the country. One of my favorite annual events is judging our
local Intel science fair and supporting young women scientists. Giving
back to young women can be a great way of remembering the bigger
picture.*

GIRL DRAMA HAPPENS, DON'T GIVE IN

I could probably write an entire book dedicated to the interpersonal conflicts with which graduate school is laden. But it will
suffice to say that a strong sense of self and all the supports you
create for yourself will be key. Okay, sometimes it might take
some Ben & Jerry's, but those days are fewer and far in between.
It is important to remember there will be good weeks and bad
weeks, and, in the end, it all averages out. Keeping a healthy perspective can prevent you from getting wrapped up in dramatic
nonsense.

I recall one particular week early on my first year in graduate school. After the initial shock of being hundreds of miles
from home sank in, my excitement started to pique. The more
I learned about my program, the classes I'd get to take, clinical
rotation possibilities, the more excited I became. I was even happy to take the statistics sequence as it was apparently the hardest part of the curriculum. In my head, the sooner I did it, the
sooner it was over. I was walking on campus one day when one
of fourth year students walked up to me and asked how graduate

school was starting off. Wonderful, I exclaimed. I felt prepared as I'd spent undergrad buried in research labs, advising, being president of a student group and so forth. In terms of my responsibilities, graduate school sounded like a bit of a break from my hectic schedule, I explained. And that did it. Not possible, she told me matter-of-factly. When she took the course, she studied 20 hours per week for stats alone aside from the other courses I'd be taking. Also, my advisor would be piling on extra duties and, frankly, graduate school was just going to be impossible. I walked away dazed, with my spirits dampened. But then a thought dawned on me. I remembered she'd been in graduate school for some time and still hadn't even proposed her Master's thesis yet. Maybe she wasn't the strongest judge of my ability level. The truth is, the naysayers will always be the harshest and make their message known.

Another student later that same week told me that graduate school would become progressively harder and harder each year even though the number of activities I had to do would decrease. She was in her seventh year of graduate school. Enough said. I didn't appreciate being a fresh-faced student being told about the misery that awaited me. What kind of welcome was that? Truth be told, these women likely had no malicious intent but were singing the mournful songs of the burnt out. The take home message is that the horrors that both students warned me of never came to fruition. Yes, graduate school is a rollercoaster ride with many ups and downs, but it really isn't that bad. It can be a pretty wonderful time. Trust me, I'm the one standing on the other side with a Ph.D. in hand!

With such a reception from the upper year students, it can be easy to get discouraged. I recall in graduate school my cohort was pretty small. It was just myself and two others. One of them left the program, and the other became a friend of mine. Throughout graduate school I was regularly on the hunt for more friends. As incoming (and larger) cohorts entered, I was hopeful at the prospect of meeting my academic best friends and counterparts.

I also felt motivated to mentor the next generation of scholars the right way without all the scare tactics. I befriended many that came after me, and met some of the most amazing and talented women I've ever met. When my undergrad therapy clients bemoan their lack of connectivity to their peers, I often let them in on a secret—in the next phases of life such as graduate school, the best is yet to come. Some of the funniest, smartest, and classiest women I've met entered my life through graduate school.

That said, it wasn't always a walk in the park. Cliques still happen in graduate school believe it or not. While one of my best friends was the anti-clique queen (meaning she invited everyone and anyone to events), not everyone was quite so open-minded. It makes sense that the young single girls clustered off together. Those who entered school later or were married grouped off as well. The wine and cheese stats studiers wound up together too. The shame in this was that many larger networks that could have formed did not. To be honest, there were some girls who I always wanted to be friends with and it never quite happened. But who knows, perhaps I came off as a completely obnoxious person to them! C'est la vie, right?

I will say though that in speaking with countless women in graduate programs, no one wants the drama, and sometimes it happens anyway. Making a choice to change that culture matters. A few years into my program, one of my colleagues and I approached our chair at the time to make a "graduate school buddies" program. Based off of similar programs in medical schools where there are "big sibs" and "little sibs," where an older student mentors and supports an incoming student, we set out to create a pilot program. We found volunteer mentors and paired each incoming student with one. While we were hoping to get larger support from the chair and department at large, the message was less than motivational. It basically amounted to, "Life's tough, they'll get used to it." Perhaps his generation of scholars did things differently. Maybe it was the old boys' club so there was little trouble in the first place. I can only speculate as to why such a program was not seen as valuable. In the end, it was an honest effort between myself and my co-program facilitator. I hope that one day departments across the country can see the value of connecting peers and providing support. When these networks form, their reach and impact is beyond measurement. However, that doesn't have to stop women and their colleagues from earnest attempts to change these cultures from within.

Your Turn!

★ *PhDeconstruct: Don't spend time worrying about the criticisms of others or trying to please everyone. Don't internalize the negative messages of others or the culture of complaining. Instead, think critically about where these messages are coming from and if there is any truth behind these messages. Are things truly miserable? Probably not. Are you doomed to fail? No. Our minds work in mysterious ways, where we are quick to listen to negative messages while discounting the positive. We don't think that maybe the person telling us how terrible things are is drowning in a stack of ungraded papers, newly divorced, or has other things going on that is heavily influencing their perspective. Don't believe everything you hear. Instead, critically deconstruct their messages and decide for yourself where the truth lies.*

GRADUATE SCHOOL AS AN ALTERNATE REALITY UNIVERSE

The alternate reality paradigm is possibly one of the most common ones I use when working with graduate students in therapy. They come to session confused, sometimes feeling they are drifting, unable to pinpoint what feels "off." They just know they are not their old selves, lack motivation, and don't know what they want anymore. I often explain this is perfectly natural. Graduate school in many ways is like an alternate reality universe. The rules are somewhere between college and "the real world," although neither entirely apply. You can sleep in until noon if you wanted and hang out in bars typically without the heavy drinking of youth. The dating scene can feel like high school all over again, and you aren't exactly "employed" but don't welcome the job market with the current economy either. You read about a saturated market where the top Ph.D. graduates don't have jobs. Adjunct faculty members are being paid poorly and then there was the devastating story the adjunct who died homeless and without access to adequate healthcare. So there's the question of what exactly you are doing with your life and why you are doing it.

Nothing about graduate school is "normal." The sooner you internalize this, the more mentally prepared you are for the inevitable ups and downs. Babysitting your advisor's son while she attends a faculty meeting? Not out of the ordinary. Realizing you and your best friend were both just hit on by the same guy in the same week? Typical. Learning your slightly difficult student's father is on the board of trustees or a major donor to the research fund you are applying to? I'm not surprised. And then there are all those ads on your internet browser that ask you if you'd like to go to technical school or get an online Ph.D. Yeah, no.

The scenarios may be endless, but there are two key ways the alternate reality universe paradigm helps. First, it banishes expectations. When you finally let go of how things are expected to proceed, unforeseen circumstances throw you off a little bit less. For example, my Master's thesis defense occurred around the time of the swine flu epidemic. As a result, my advisor who was the committee chair was essentially quarantined and he called in to the meeting remotely. Hours of preparation for any question never prepares you for your chair being ill. Acceptance that very bizarre things may happen also makes it easier to laugh when they do. During one of my training years I had a client with scabies. Of course, I had a student with scabies in a tiny closet office that had to be fumigated. Why wouldn't that happen to me? When viewed in the right light, it was actually somewhat funny in retrospect.

In addition to freeing one from expectations, the alternate reality paradigm helps one gain acceptance and flexibility to establish one's own set of norms. For example, graduate school is unique in that, unlike medical school or law school where everyone's requirements are nearly identical and spelled out far in advance, this is far from the case. New requirements or classes never listed in the bulletin appear, your program is supposed to be entirely unique and its nuances apply to only you. While a medical student is unlikely to have someone call them on their cell phone to ask them to send that abstract or come into lab on the weekend, a graduate student is very likely to have these encounters. In fact, a lack of boundaries is a key distinguishing factor in graduate school. You don't have the same type of privacy. Your time is regarded differently and the expectations of you can run on a 24-hour cycle.

While you cannot control the external conditions of graduate school, you can be very strategic in drafting and determining what you do and don't want out of graduate school. After all, during orientation isn't that what the program director comes in and tells you? This is the time for you to flourish and think of every day as professional development, they say. If your advisor affords you basic flexibilities, you might get to decide what classes to take and when to take them.

This will sound atrocious. But I will share it anyway. As someone who is not a morning person and who was at times frightened by the arctic Midwest conditions, I avoided both early morning classes and ones located in the quad furthest from me. Somehow, I managed to meet all course requirements without any classes that started earlier than maybe 9-10am-ish and never had to trek out into the snow for longer than 10-15 minute intervals. Oh and of course, I generally had Fridays free. Point being, when in an alternate universe, why not make up your own rules to your own advantage if they are not significantly harming you or anyone else? From my perspective, saving myself from pneumonia was doing everyone a favor.

The idea is when the rules are constantly changing or unstated in the first place, make up some of your own (reasonably). My final year in graduate school I was applying and interviewing for clinical internships. Since I knew travel might be involved and wanted to stay healthy, I decided to make sure I was eating enough. During stressful times I was prone to being chronically underweight and hence became sick quickly. So every day was homemade French toast day. It was divine. And I knew it'd only be this one year in my life that I'd get to live this way. I think my arteries are okay, as I actually found a pretty healthy and nutritious recipe. Still, it can be fun to play around with some of the flexibilities that graduate school can offer. Again, it's about getting creative. This might be the last time you can host weekly movie nights and everyone lives a building down from you or the only time you can keep the late hours that one with a 9-5 could never do.

Your Turn!

★ *PhDelineate: Go ahead, make up some of your own rules. Delineate a few staples that might up your productivity and fun. For example, make a commitment to a regular exercise schedule on some days of the week and days when you can stay home in pjs doing some light reading and catching up on episodes of your favorite TV show. All things in moderation, of course, but don't be afraid to test the waters a bit.*

CHAPTER 8

THE 3 "P"S IN PH.D.

"If you want the rainbow, you've got to put up with the rain."
—Dolly Parton

PERSEVERANCE: DISILLUSIONMENT, ROMANCE AND WHY AM I HERE AGAIN?

There are many times throughout the graduate school process that one faces waves of disillusionment. As the years go by, these waves may become more frequent. Often for those with children or who entered graduate school later in life, time may feel to be even more of the essence. There may be family demands on time on top of academic ones. Furthermore, if you are single and hoping to be coupled, you may be watching the years go by as your friends with balanced lives and jobs meet people and get married. Meanwhile, your longest term commitment to date has been your dissertation document.

Perseverance matters because the number of factors that may distract you can be plentiful. I once saw a therapy client who first came to treatment because she was single and wanting to get married. Then once she was married she was upset about not getting pregnant. She kept pushing aside the larger issues of her degree completion and channeling her frustration over her academic challenges into her other life plans. Of course, it was wonderful that she had managed to find some balance and healthy relationships during graduate school. However, she was also escaping her reality as a graduate student as well. It's all about finding balance.

Additionally, I think it's necessary to provide a few words for my single readers who may be navigating this challenging patch of pursuing their degrees and relationships. The nature and topic of romantic relationships in graduate school is a highly complex one. Interspersed in the graduate school rollercoaster, it brings hopes, joys, and a glimpse of normality and happiness in an ordinary life. And yet, added to the burden of an overbearing advisor and unwieldy data can be cause for some of the greatest devastation known to womankind.

What is unique to graduate school relationships has an awful lot to do with timing. This is a time when our friends from our grad school and non-grad school life get married and have children. Happily. The my-Facebook-profile-picture-will-be-a-professional-wedding-shot-for-the-next-two-years type of happy. For those of us without the glow of love and/or pregnancy, the constant bombardment of the route we have forgone is a regular slap in the face. And it is frustrating. While women enter graduate school with the intent of advancing their careers and professional knowledge, gnawing away at the back of their mind is often the same thought: "Wouldn't it be so wonderful if I found my spouse right here in graduate school?"

It is that fanciful escape. That you'd have a partner for all those special graduate school family and "couples" events. That you'd know even if all this schooling did not work out, you'd still be happy with a husband and kids if that's your cup of tea. That he (or she) would share your values, be educated, and it would end in happily ever after. In truth, I got caught in that fantasy more than once over several years. Perhaps I was going through a rough patch. I missed my family and the idea of creating one of my own was a constant comfort I kept at the back of my mind.

Coming from a culture where marriage and kids are a given, I found myself thinking about the prospect of a relationship more and more.

This is not at all to say that being open-minded to relationships is bad. On the contrary, openness is a great thing. It is not so beneficial though when graduate student women become preoccupied, see this as the solution to one's problems, or engage in relationships haphazardly (i.e., with someone who is not actually a good match).

But as I've said before, graduate school can play some tricky mind games on us. Again, it is never just one factor. It is the culmination of stressors, lack of environmental control, social context, and more. We are not always ourselves and that is how we later remember our missteps with embarrassment. I tell my clients over and over they are not to blame. They acted as anyone would in an unfamiliar and stressful situation. It is as one of my colleagues would say *a perfectly normal response to an abnormal situation*. And graduate school is just that. It is an abnormal situation. It is like a temporary haze you are in, somewhere between childhood and adulthood. You are just trying to make sense of it, create meaning, and hopefully graduate with a degree.

What often happens though is a blind leading the blind situation. Those with no relationship of their own try to guide you through it. Their efforts are earnest and out of goodwill. But they are just as clueless as you. And suddenly you find yourself on dates with guys you know you'd never date, dancing with strangers whose names you may not remember tomorrow, and any number of other things you will later regret. It is okay. I have counseled many women with similar concerns, and awareness is once again the first step.

It can be easy to compare. Blame your lack of happiness on the fact that you don't have x, y, or z that so-and-so over there has. The irony is that we are all envious of the thing we don't have. The married woman wishes she could be included in more of the single girls' activities and feels isolated. The single woman wishes she had someone to come home to at night. Accepting ourselves where we are and loving ourselves as is becomes so important here.

Allowing our diva side to come out is a self-preservation move. Get that manicure or massage, buy that new outfit, get your highlights re-done, and opt for that tinted moisturizer that will have you out the door faster than primer, moisturizer, and foundation! Take care of yourself however that looks. You are your biggest advocate, and your loudest cheerleader. You should celebrate yourself and focus on your many amazing qualities. Forget the pity party for the things you've forgone or the parts that you wish you could re-do. You have the here and now, and as the Buddhists and Taoists would say, that is all that really matters. Perseverance is often a matter of attitude. So don't lose hope, whatever you may feel like you are missing out on.

Your Turn!

★ *PhDamsels: Don't be a damsel in distress! Write the ending to your own fairytale. Don't stress about all that's passing you by. Live in the here and now. Distractions may be plentiful. Perhaps you've gone from dreaming of a Ph.D. to an MRS degree. But have you ever watched an episode of The Bachelor? There are aspiring models, actresses, nannies and hair stylists in their 30s crying their eyes out saying they are running out of time to find "the one." But did you really come to graduate school to find "the one" in the first place? Did you come to graduate school so you could buy a house and have a garden? No, likely you came for the education and other goals started capturing your attention. There is nothing wrong with those goals, but there is a time and place for everything. It can also help to find postgrad role models. I had a good friend whose advisor found her life partner post grad school, another whose mother gave birth to her at age 37. Collecting these stories not only gave me hope, but were also normalizing and inspirational. It reminded me to focus on one thing at a time, believe a bit more in fate, and have faith that all would work out in time, even if wasn't exactly with the speed I wanted.*

PROCRASTINATION PITFALLS: HINT— GET OFF FACEBOOK

I would be remiss if I did not include a reference to a very important concept at this stage of graduate school—efficiency. While lack of efficiency can become fuel for anxiety, the entire point of it is just the opposite. It's not about getting sloppy or speeding through things carelessly. It's about objectively evaluating the merits of spending excessive amounts of time in one domain versus another. As I've emphasized throughout this book, you will most certainly come to a crossroads where something has to give. Otherwise, you risk losing your sanity and possibly even health. It's about figuring out what shortcuts are appropriate, when to take the easier road, and when it's worth going all out for a project or paper.

I often challenge my therapy clients when I ask them what it would be like if for a week they took on the mindset of a "slacker." What would it be like? For my highly Type A clients to whom I suggest this, it means still getting all the work done, but with about half of the stress. Perfectionism is in their blood. Letting go of a little bit of their standards and expectations saves much grief on their part. So don't be afraid to experiment with doing a little bit less. Don't revise the abstract 10 times. It is only supposed to be 150 words anyway. Stop obsessing about the numerous permutations of ways you can state the same exact thing. Skim through a few of the 10 articles you have to read before class. Pick up the highlights, pay attention to the methods and results, but don't necessarily worry about the history of how a measure came to be. Of course, please don't take my suggestion as permission to violate copyright, or do anything unlawful or academically dishonest. My point is that the little things add up.

Deciding what to prioritize and what to let go of can be key. Many time management experts will use the following quadrant to help assess priorities and the order in which tasks need to be completed. Based off of Stephen Covey's book *The 7 Habits of Highly Effective People*, the following quadrant matrix helps assess the urgency versus importance of needs to help prioritize tasks. Think about the following matrix sitting on a scatterplot. As you move toward the right, urgency goes from low to high. As you move up, importance moves from low to high. You can see then that high urgency and high importance items translate to the "critical activities" portion of the quadrant, while the lowest urgency and importance is the "distractions" category.

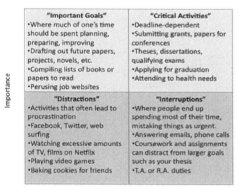

I've talked about my refusal to go into lab in other parts of this book. My point was that it was inefficient. Getting ready to go to lab means getting up, showered, dressed, packing a lunch, and transporting oneself to and from lab. All those steps are wasting precious minutes. By rolling out of bed, powering up my laptop while eating breakfast I got tons more done (don't worry, I still showered). In fact, I was possibly working for more hours than my labrat counterparts. I often also worked well into the night, though many in lab settings would call it a day once the clock hit 5 PM. But as anyone knows, graduate school is not a 9-5 endeavor. We could have entered the "real world" if we'd wanted that. It may sound like my approach in many ways is the breeding ground for a workaholic work style. In all honesty, the nerd in me loves my field and isn't desperately running away from it the minute the clock hits 5. I will say though that working around the clock can often aid one in getting things done faster and can increase efficiency. Many study skills specialists often advocate working in blocks to decrease fatigue and help with concentration. In my "off" blocks from working, I'd clean house, do my laundry, run, and find ways of obtaining better balance and gaining more time. It may not be the popular approach, but any diva knows there will be haters.

Your Turn!

★ *PhDistractions: Say goodbye to distractions and hello to efficiency, ease, and a greater sense of calm accomplishment. Use the quadrant provided above to prioritize your daily and weekly activities. Think long-term and realistically. And remember, tasks that need to get done are not always work-related. There is a balance between the spotless house and a total wreck. Prioritize not only your academic tasks, but don't neglect the importance of a clean living environment that will help you feel at peace. The same goes for exercise and other fitness activities that will energize you and help you get more done.*

FOR PANIC BUTTON PRESS HERE

I've had the unfortunate occasion to work with more than one graduate student while they were being dismissed from their academic program. By the time they made their way to my office, it was too little too late. In many circumstances these students could have chosen to "stop out" as occurred at Stanford University or take a leave which was far more common at UC Berkeley than I'd ever imagine. Having come from a pretty traditional graduate school myself, it was rare that I heard of students taking leaves. Usually, they just left the department all together. While I've touched on this concept earlier in this book, I want to take some time in walking you through some of the resources and tools of which you should be aware.

Depending upon the university, there are any number of types of leaves. There are academic withdrawals, medical withdrawals, and even retroactive withdrawals (I know, kind of sounds like Harry Potter-style magic). At some schools all types of leaves are clustered together into one category, whereas other colleges and universities might separate them out. Certainly they take some paperwork and can be tedious; as someone who has provided mental health documentation for students filing these petitions, I know how drawn out they can be. But I also know that for the student I worked with who suffered a severe psychotic break, the deans and directors got involved and expedited the entire process. So essentially, there are different levels of this.

The important thing that should go without saying is to be knowledgeable and ethical. The number of students who attempted to claim "emotional distress" or wanted a letter out of me to justify a therapy animal was unfortunate as it took away from the students truly in need. And frankly, too often it was those students in need who didn't even know what resources were available to them. Hence, if you're the student who is tempted to skim past this section because it doesn't apply to you, you might actually be the one who should keep reading.

Depending upon the school there might be varying limits for types of leaves. For example, at Stanford there was no limit to how many times you could leave and return. At other schools, after a certain number of petitions for withdrawals, you were walking risky territory. You could risk getting onto the ladder of academic admonishments which range from warning status to expulsion. Knowing the rungs of this ladder as scary as it may seem can alleviate quite a bit of anxiety. I worked with a woman once who, due to several unfortunate life circumstances, was starting to slip in school. She was nearly hysterical in tears as she was already on probation and another poor term could be the end of her road. After consulting with our counseling center director, though, I learned that she was really on the first rung of the ladder. Granted, this does not mean one should ever take these things lightly. It is important to know the steps and too often students are completely in the dark when all they have to do is ask an advisor or dean for information.

For international students, a whole other set of rules and regulations may apply. I worked with my fair share of international graduate students for whom not doing well academically could mean being ousted out of the country. Sometimes students would apply the rules of their homelands to the U.S. assuming they had more or less chances than they truly had. If they had communicated and stayed in consistent communication with their advisors and deans, they would have saved quite a few headaches.

The take home message is that you can in fact take a leave and still walk out with a Ph.D. in hand. Too many students are frightened of even looking into the possibility of a personal leave or medical withdrawal. They fret internally or their health is deteriorating and they assume their only option is to leave permanently. Since we rarely hear about these cases, or they are so hushed in secrecy when they do occur, we are not given the opportunity to learn from similar cases with peers. In graduate school I knew of a handful of students who left the program during my tenure. But I can barely recite the reasons why they left. They were all capable, doing well in classes from what I was seeing. But clearly, something was off. A more open dialogue about this could decrease attrition rates and enhance overall quality of life factors. So if things aren't going well and you truly might need a break, don't panic! There is a button you could press to get some help.

Your Turn!

★ *PhDigress: It's okay to wander off onto the beaten road. Robert Frost wrote in his renown poem that he took the road less traveled, and it was that which made all the difference. For some, graduate school may be a hurling train bustling through tunnels at a dizzying pace. For others, there are stops and starts. While throughout this book I have emphasized an efficient way of completing graduate school, this should never come at the expense of your personal health and well-being. Maybe you need a break for a semester to re-assess why you even came to graduate school. Perhaps it's not graduate school per se that is the problem, but you aren't in the correct field. I've known students to move from psychology to communications, or genetics to linguistics. The avid pursuit and passion for knowledge is there, but somehow along the journey they found themselves on the wrong path, only to be sparked by another road entirely. Don't be afraid to give yourself a break and try something new for a while. You never know, maybe that will be what will have made all the difference.*

CHAPTER 9

PHINISHED!

"Once made equal to man, woman becomes his superior."
—*Socrates*

GETTING THE MOST OF WHAT YOU CAME FOR

In graduate school, many times I came across the ambiguously graduating student. You know the one—they were supposed to have graduated who knows how many semesters ago. Each time you see them in passing and inquire about their progress, they "plan" to graduate the very next semester. And yet, lo and behold, they are still around as they were from the day you arrived fresh-faced as a first-year student. Sometimes this is more the advisor's doing than anything. The student is cheap labor and graduating that student means losing them and time as they would have to train a brand new student all over again. Other times, the student starts dillydallying or is in denial of a very real fact. Soon they will be on the job market or have to start applying to post-doctoral positions. This means they need to start making some big life decisions and start doing so pretty quickly.

One of the advantages (but also stressful parts) of professional-style programs is that the next step is very clearly defined. For example, in clinical and counseling psychology, the next natural step is a clinical internship with a lengthy process and magical match process that may bump you halfway across the country to train at a site you may or may not have cared for much in the first place. But once those wheels are set in motion, it is very clear when you must propose and defend your dissertation and all the other parts fall into place. In other words, there is a deadline. An endpoint. You know, the part when you ... stop.

While the next step can be terrifying for some, it can also be a very exciting time. At this stage, you are finally an "advanced" graduate student (whatever that means exactly), which also means you have enough seniority to call some of the shots. I recall when waiting for my match results I knew there was a very real possibility I would not match at all. A quarter of students were not getting placed anywhere nationwide due to a placement shortage. That's when I came up with the back-up plan.

It helps to think, whether you are on the job market or applying for any next step, what you wanted to get out of graduate school. Taking an inventory of your earliest ambitions can be critical. After four or more years of intensive study, shifting priorities and endless projects, sometimes it can be hard to have a clear mind about the matter. You might be thinking, "all I want is a way out!" But realistically, from day one, you may have fantasized about all sorts of things—teaching your own class, applying for and receiving a grant, mentoring younger students. While you get the wheels in motion for the next step of your journey, assess if there is anything left you can do to maximize your time and experiences.

When I started off in graduate school, I had been approached about co-teaching a seminar for Notre Dame's Center for Social Concerns. It was called Children in Poverty. The subject matter, the opportunity to teach a small seminar-style class, travel to New York to meet with agencies sounded like a dream opportunity. Yet, due to numerous demands, I had to decline at that time. However, I never forgot about my desire to pursue that incredible teaching and learning experience. Then, when due to a twist of fate, my good friend was one of the co-teachers for that very class, I approached her to see if I could co-teach with her. When she said yes, I immersed myself in the subject matter that had piqued my curiosity early on. I also became interested in doing more with the class, possibly even creating new courses. Had I not gone onto an internship, I had some exciting opportunities that I could still take advantage of. Hence, my back-up plan, and a very exhilarating one at that.

Much like the priorities quadrant I shared in an earlier chapter, it is also important to prioritize the bigger goals you set for yourself in graduate school. Maybe you wanted a certain number of publications, or to present at a prestigious conference. Trying to do everything will be overwhelming and can lead to burnout. It can help to have those that are the must-haves, and those that are in the category of "wouldn't it be great if…" The latter category would be the cherry on top, but let's not forget you're already getting the ice cream and whipped cream to start. That's more than enough to sate my appetite.

Your Turn!

★ *PhDelight: This is the fun part! You have completed the primary requirements, have figured out the lay of the land, and created a wonderful community of friends. It is almost like living the good life of retirement in graduate school. Being near the very end doesn't mean giving up or haphazardly throwing things together so you can quickly leave. Relish your final year(s). Dream big and think about those last things you really wanted to do while in graduate school. Find a way and make them happen.*

JUST SAY NO!

During the writing of this book, I pored over the most important factors to highlight and mention, noting it would be impossible to cover everything. This was actually not unlike what I've said about overreaching in graduate school. However, as I went through this process, I had a realization. While naturally much of the guidance coming from this book stems from the experiences of my colleagues, patients, and, of course, myself, it is highly colored through my lens. I was quite fortunate to have a wonderful graduate school experience (hence writing this book!) and much of my guidance comes from this perspective.

As we know, not all fare so well due to any number of circumstances. To make sure there weren't any final critical topics I'd neglected to address, I surveyed my female colleagues and fellow members of the Ph.D. club during the writing of this guide. I asked what they thought was the most crucial piece of advice to include in such a book. While everything they mentioned has been covered in these pages, there was one particular point for which there was unanimous and overwhelming support: Learn to say no.

As someone who was fortunate to be pretty independent and lab-less in graduate school, I was rarely approached, pressured, and so forth. There were not a plethora of elective research opportunities constantly in my face. This is probably why I didn't give much thought to this point. For most graduate students, though, the opportunities can feel endless. Numerous projects, papers, books, presentations all vying for their attention. I have noted previously that as women we are often raised to be people-pleasers and to say yes. Although in just the preceding section I encourage readers to do a little bit of everything they wanted, there is also a caveat. Do it for yourself.

Don't make your goals about pleasing and impressing others. This can be very difficult to do. After all, a first-author publication is pleasing both to ourselves and faculty recruitment committees. But sometimes, the desire to say yes to every opportunity can mean missing out on something better to come later on. It may also mean you are not being true to your own values and interests. During my career, many times opportunities emerged that looked amazing on paper but did not align with my inherent needs. Sometimes I took them, only to be disinterested and unhappy later on. So I learned to let go if things did not feel right. It can take some time to learn to trust your intuition. You might be tempted by numerous opportunities for some time until saying no becomes essential to your survival.

While my perspective throughout graduate school was influenced by a number of demographic factors, one that bears heavily on my sense of time was being single. I did not have mouths to feed, diapers to change, a partner or husband to attend to, on top of other responsibilities. For many graduate student moms, saying yes to that extra research project can mean saying no to children's soccer games or simply time spent with the family. Though graduate school is important, it is by no means more important than precious time spent with loved ones. Learning to say no to work commitments can mean learning to say yes to a more fulfilled and well-rounded life.

Your Turn!
★ *PhDevotion: Remain devoted to the best interests of yourself and your family. Devote yourself fully to the tasks you sign up for, but don't spread yourself too thin. It is better to accomplish a few things with depth and complexity, rather than waste time on numerous superficial contributions that just eat away at your time. Don't feel guilty, apologetic, or compare yourself to your peers. Another cliché thing I'm going to say due to its veracity—remain true to yourself because that really is what matters the most. It's not about your advisor's career, but yours. It can be easy to forget that, but helps to remind yourself.*

SAYING GOODBYE CAN BE THE HARDEST THING
The graduate school journey is one that truly spans over a decade at the least. Some find their way to a Ph.D. by a twist of

fate, and for others it has been in the stars for many years. Undergraduate years lay the foundation, and even after the degree is received, the experiences and memories from this time remain forever. For some, undergraduate years become "the glory days." For others, it may be graduate school. It is during that time after all that they finally get to fully dive deeply into the ocean of their chosen field. There are difficult periods, be they weeks or even months. But little compares to the experience of being hooded and officially joining the academy with full regalia in a historic tradition.

Saying goodbye is the part of graduate school that is rarely discussed. An academic career in particular can closely mimic graduate school itself such that it becomes akin to an extended resort stay (not quite, but you know what I mean). As we have established, graduate school can be a difficult to define period in one's life. One is still a student, of adult age, but not yet in the adult world. Further, being a student comes with its privileges, and I'm not just talking about the student discounts. You might brush off mistakes, errors in judgment, and ruptured relationships as a side effect of graduate school. You don't take full blame for things because you were under pressure, a deadline, and in dramatic times, life going nowhere.

Graduating means you are suddenly thrust into a world with your peers who wound up with very different lives. You barely have a savings account and likely some student debt. Meanwhile your high school and college classmates who went straight into the workforce have been working for a decade and maybe even own their own homes. At the very least, they have a real couch and not a futon, and an actual box designated for holding their Christmas decorations. Maybe they are in middle management and pulling a salary higher than what your post-doc or even first position might pay. These are dismal realizations, but in this economy are not out of the realm of the possible. On the flip side, by entering and now exiting graduate school however, you have effectively maximized your odds for a plethora of options, many of which you might not even be consciously aware of now. Though networks will come into play on the job market, graduate study does enable you to effectively skip steps that many without such degrees simply cannot. During my fellowship year, I applied for a director position at an elite small liberal arts college. They were thrilled at my application and quite eager to bring me on board. Were it not for a timing issue, my first position out of graduate school could have been a rather prestigious gig. The candidate who wound up with the position had worked in the field for years, but without a Ph.D., before finally landing this spot.

However, the true difficulties of graduating do not revolve around jobs and entering the adult world entirely. The shift from graduate student to working professional is also one of identity. Who are you when you are no longer a student? What does it mean when you don't have someone telling you what your goals should be? I'll get into the story of my own post-graduate career path in the final chapter of this book. But a wise adage that stands out from the period when I was contemplating my own life path—it came from a social media post. A friend had written about the woes of unemployment, about trying to use the time to find herself and clarify her professional goals. A colleague of hers had written a very poignant comment in return. She wrote that after years of being buried in research, clinical placements, having an academic advisor say one thing and a practicum supervisor say another, she had effectively lost her own voice and her way. She was so used to blindly jumping through hoop after hoop that it took her some time to figure out exactly what she wanted. For the first time in years, she was finally… free.

It is easy for so many years to have tunnel vision. There is one goal at hand and that is degree completion. It can be effortless to lose sight of the bigger picture. Why did you come to graduate school again? What were those goals? On top of that, things may have shifted significantly. Maybe you entered graduate school expecting you'd love teaching only to realize that standing up in front of a classroom scares the living daylights out of you. At the same time, doing something different from what you were trained for can seem terrifying. I would say the overwhelming majority of students I've encountered in Ph.D. programs enter graduate school with plans of becoming tenure-track faculty and leave with a very different idea.

According to an article in the *Chronicle on Higher Education* by Mary Ann Mason (2012), professor and co-director of the Berkeley Law Center on Health, Economic & Family Security and the former dean of their Graduate School, several important forces are at play with respect to shifting goals. In the first place, tenure track positions are becoming more and more rare. The National Center for Education Statistics in 2007 reported that only 31% of faculty were tenured and tenure-track. With the overwhelming trend toward academics taking part-time and adjunct positions, this is understandable. In fact, another article ran in the *Chronicle* discussing the preference for some faculty in obtaining such positions as they enabled them to focus on their love of teaching rather than staying afloat in a publish-or-perish setting where their passion would be put on the backburner. Regardless, women in particular are finding tenure-track positions to be less and less appealing. According to Mason, "In a survey we conducted of all doctoral students at the University of California, more than 70% of women and over half of all men said they considered a career at a research university to be too hard-driving and unfriendly to family life." Furthermore, only 11% of new moms in the study still maintained their goal of wanting to be research professors even though 46% of them started out with the same aim.

This isn't to say that everyone's goals change. But for many folks they do, and, believe it or not, altering ideas of what one wants in the future takes some coping. You used to envision the future looking one way, and now that picture has changed. It takes wrapping your head around changes. And as we know, change means loss. But it also means of a whole new gain. Furthermore, the incredible part of graduating means you are no longer truly bound to any one thing for an extended period of time. You can try out different positions and different places and nothing truly astronomical will happen. Yet even entertaining such thoughts can take some getting used to.

Another reality of graduating means saying goodbye to people and places. Ultimately, it is up to you whether you sever ties or keep bonds alive from a distance. When I was getting ready to graduate ahead of some of my peers, I was excited to do all sorts of activities with them for the last time. However, not all of them were feeling the same way. We all handle goodbyes and grieving in different ways. While I wanted to make the most of things, some friends wanted to avoid this inevitable reality all together. Others were drowning in their workload too deeply to have any time. In the end, some of the friendships I maintained and others became more distant. I still love and care for so many of those that were an integral part of my life. But I also learned the tough lesson that the phone works both ways, and that I could only initiate so many phone calls and meetings before I was pursuing a one-sided friendship. This too is its own transition.

Graduating also means saying goodbye to trusted advisors and mentors. In some cases you may remain collaborators. At other times you are bidding them adieu for one final time. It is important, though, whether they be your advisor or not, to maintain such mentorship relationships throughout your career. I will admit that I used to roll my eyes at the idea of mentorship. I've yet to ever meet someone whose identical life I would want.

So why would I be taking advice from them I'd wonder. As it turns out, they can open up your eyes to many new and real possibilities. And having a mentor does not mean turning into their clone or protégé.

When I was debating a clinical versus academic career, my supervisor and training director at Berkeley asked me to share my hesitations toward pursuing a clinical route. I shared with him my fears of burnout, the fact that, although I love seeing patients, I couldn't see myself holed up in an office all day. I wanted to go to academic conferences and continue learning. I also wanted a more flexible schedule than a traditional 9 to 5. Somehow I had equated a clinical career with saying goodbye to all of that. He showed me how this did not have to be the case. He shared examples of clinical staff who were still engaged in research. He was on editorial boards and attended our national convention yearly, and, through supervision and training, was able to stay fresh in clinical literature while giving back to the next generation of scholars. To top it off, by shifting his patient schedule around a bit, he had a free day on Mondays when he often went to movies and had more time with family and friends. Had I not opened myself up to his mentorship and influence, I would not have been aware of all the routes that lay before me.

While graduating and moving onto your next post might mean moving away from trusted mentors, it can be important to find new professionals and seniors in your field with whom to connect. Of course, you can still use email and phone calls to connect with old advisors, but there is something about going for coffee or lunch face to face that can feel much different and highly supportive. Joining alumni clubs can also be an excellent factor to consider for both finding mentors and fellow professionals. Sometimes it can be hard to connect socially with peers who didn't quite make the same types of sacrifices you did or who simply seem to live very different lives. I've had more than one conversation with individuals who sounded shocked that I didn't have any children at my age. Sometimes no explanation can suffice in these circumstances. Naturally, this doesn't mean you'll be a social pariah. But it can help to check your expectations when going off into the "real world" (never to be mistaken with the MTV show).

Regarding expectations, in fact, it would help to get rid of them completely. For many years I watched my colleagues ahead of me graduate and wind up in a variety of positions. Most had post-docs and a few landed some teaching positions at smaller colleges. I also witnessed roommates who were law students and neighbors with MBAs go off with markedly different prospects at times. There was the one roommate who wound up at one of New York's most prestigious law firms, and the MBA graduate who managed to live in Greenwich after landing a first job. There were those who stayed locally and those that temporarily gave up the career and had babies instead. There are so many countless paths that it can be impossible to know exactly what will happen to any given person. This is where the tricky concept of fate comes in. Being open to whatever happens and maintaining an attitude of gratitude can help you make the best of what unfolds.

I recall after graduating I was talking with one of my best friends about elite schools. We spoke about how tough it was for us to leave Notre Dame knowing no school would ever measure up for us. From the picturesque campus to the polite and well-mannered students and, of course, the spirit and traditions, we were quite sad that we could never capture that again. In our minds we planned trips back to campus, fantasized about finding jobs there and re-creating all that was. But as the seasons teach us, there is constant change and no two snowflakes will ever fall quite the same. It took some grieving for us to let go of this reality, but it was an emotional process critical for us to have. Though you spend much of grad school looking with anticipation toward the future, the future arrives and suddenly the safety of the past looks far more welcoming. It can take some time to realize what incredible possibilities really do lay before you. I've seen countless graduate students cross over to the other side that is graduation, possibly stumble over a brief step, but then get up radiant and glowing. They refer to graduations as a commencement because they really do signify a beginning, and the start of something truly amazing at that.

Your Turn!

★ *PhDivine: Recognize the divinity in all that you have accomplished and how far you have come! The journey is finally at an end. Find your way special way to say goodbye but to also cherish the moments you had. Though social media can have its problems, it can be a great way of connecting with colleagues. I can't tell you how many times I announced going to a conference and learning that an old colleague would be there. Over the years I've probably seen a half dozen beloved colleagues at conferences and simply through learning they landed a position nearby. Phone calls, cards, emails help keep connections alive, so don't be shy about it. Find out if there is a local alumni club and consider joining it. Maybe plan to take a trip back to campus with friends and have a mini-reunion. But also remember that things will have to change and learn to embrace the new. Do what had always been impossible because of graduate school. Now is the time!*

Part IV

A Touch of Powder to Set

CHAPTER 10

PhDIVAS UNITE

"If you can't feed a hundred people, then just feed one."
—*Mother Theresa s*

WHAT'S NEXT?

You've walked across the stage in your fancy robes, shaken countless hands, smiled and taken the photos at campus landmarks, and said your goodbyes. What happens next? For some, they may know exactly where they are headed. Perhaps they've landed a post-doc or career position. Others may have chosen to wait for the dust to settle before committing themselves to the full-time task of finding the road that leads to their vocation.

You may consult with advisors, fellow colleagues, but ultimately the decision comes down to you. Maybe the prestigious faculty position is in a location that feels like it's in the middle of nowhere. Perhaps you have your partner's position and your children's schooling to take into account. Or you are pondering the fact that you can now go about finding a partner or have children. It can help to assess what you want knowing that this is your chance to set the stage for your future.

Very few openly discuss the job hunt process and rarely are we offered an in-depth view of what's really going on. Often you may hear about the student a few years ahead of you who found a post-doc and then a faculty post. But you don't hear about the market, the pesky little ways that job ads are written that exclude candidates. According to author and recruiter Kathleen Conners, only 5% of job applicants obtain a position through an online posting or job board; 15% obtain jobs through recruiters; 65-70% of jobs are created by small businesses; 70-85% of candidates obtain positions through networking; 85% of jobs are never advertised; and 90% of hiring managers locate candidates through their own contacts.

While these statistics pertain mainly to the general populace, they are still worth paying attention to. There is a reason why most individual's dream jobs aren't out there—they might need to be created by the organizations in the first place! Below, I've shared my twisty road to employment as it can be helpful to hear how unconventionally things really can happen. Although much of my own story has been largely private, I am a strong believer in sharing our missteps, especially if it means others can grow and learn from them.

When I graduated, I was in the middle of my clinical internship. I had already accepted a fellowship at Stanford that would ensure I receive the final 2,000 clinical hours I would need that would then qualify me to take a board exam and state jurisprudence exam. Until I was licensed, I was basically tied up. As my fellowship year neared an end, I was peppered with questions from well-meaning colleagues and supervisors about whether or not I had secured employment. I certainly understood their concern. Many of them assumed I had huge college debts to pay off, or planned to live in the atrociously priced Bay Area. But as someone who had gone straight through from undergraduate to graduate school without taking any extra years or time off, frankly, I was tired.

As one of my good friends, who is an assistant professor now in Nebraska, once said, "I want to settle down in one place and stop wondering where the darn grocery store is." You see, because both of us had lived in four cities in four years as a function of how our programs worked. We were tired of moving around, constant flights back home to visit family, buying furniture, selling it, getting stuck in Chicago O'Hare airport for the umpteenth time. It makes sense not to want to rush into another ordeal, seeing as how I was living off an extremely generous stipend of $30k in Palo Alto. As you can well envision, I had lots of discretionary funds to enable these moves to pricey areas.

I had learned at the very least that the income of a psychologist working at a university was not great, even at a full-time staff salary. Cost of living would clearly be a huge factor. I was trained for college counseling center work though. It's what I had done for the last four years. And although it was fulfilling, it was missing some bigger pieces such as outreaching to larger communities, flexibility, and autonomy. But it was safe and comfortable, and I kept getting badgered with questions about what job I was going to have after fellowship. So I applied to two counseling centers in the Pacific Northwest, and was quickly snatched up for a staff psychologist and program director position at a small private college. The staff was incredibly warm and welcoming. It was not in the best area of town, but word on the street was that it was rebuilding. They had put me up in a gorgeous hotel after all that was overlooking the water, and it was such a welcome relief from the hustle and bustle of the Bay Area.

I busily and happily made my way through studying for my licensing exams, packing up, finding an apartment to live in and so forth. But interestingly, not once did I ever officially announce the position to friends and colleagues. Later, when it was time for the move, we drove in with my parents when my father took a wrong exit. We went to my new apartment using a different route and essentially drove through a very unsafe neighborhood adjacent to my new residence. Suddenly, I started to panic. I realized that something had felt off along in the back of my mind that

I'd been pushing away. Every time that one of the leasing agents would talk about safety or that one part of town I should avoid at night, I got this nagging feeling.

I would imagine myself spending all day providing therapy, listening to difficult cases, and then coming home to an empty apartment as it would be largely unsafe to go anywhere in the evenings. As this reality sunk in, I suddenly wasn't so sure that was the life I wanted. Yes, in society we're told that's just how things are. You go to school, then you wind up in a 9 to 5 like the rest of us. But that's not why I went to graduate school. I wanted a better life, a more well-rounded one. I also wanted a better salary, something that wouldn't go nearly entirely to my rent each month. I dreamed one day of owning my own home. And that didn't feel like too much to ask for.

The prospect of living that life simply didn't align with what I wanted. If I started that cycle, I knew it would be much harder to get out. So I did something highly uncharacteristic—I declined the position at the last minute. The director was incredibly kind and asked me to reconsider. As truly warm as he and the staff were, I just knew in my heart that even if I did commit to the position it wouldn't be for very long.

I wound up returning home with absolutely no plan. I was overcome with relief but later dread. Now what? I called old connections, but nothing came of it. My home state had a pretty saturated market for psychologists. Few positions opened, they immediately went to familiar faces, and even fewer seemed to retire or leave their posts. I went through phases of being highly selective and highly desperate. Needless to say, there were lots and lots of tears. Suddenly without a professional identity and living at home with my parents I felt like a failure and was completely lost. I was mad at the jobs I was overqualified for that weren't even offering me interviews, the economy and everything in between.

Then on a whim, I remembered that at Berkeley's counseling center, a lot of folks started out as part-time contract staff until something more permanent opened up. So I emailed the director at my alma mater out of the blue and asked if she needed any psychologists. Within a week of passing my final licensing exam, I was hired on as part-time staff. Ironically, I realized it was in many ways what I'd dreamed of my last two years in California. Something light, part-time, so I could be active professionally while having some time for leisure. The position then led serendipitously to a full-time post at a group practice where everything seemed to seamlessly fall into place. I was given the salary I'd always hoped to start out at, flexibility in my schedule, and autonomy.

During my period of part-time work I made a lifelong ambition come true when I enrolled in a 200-hour yoga teacher training program. I trained for 30 hours a week over six weeks while working 20 hours. I also became a regular guest on our local morning television show and did monthly segments on mental health, my real life dream job. I toyed with private practice and realized I wasn't quite ready for it yet. I started prioritizing my personal life and establishing a network of close friendships and a community.

All of these incredible things manifested from what felt like the most miserable period in my life. I fought what was my fate for a long time until I just surrendered to it. Once I decided to make the best of my situation and actively work to take advantage of my circumstances did things fall into place. Certainly there's more stability to be had. I am positive that my career and positions will continue to morph and mold into more and more of what I've always wanted. In the meantime, I've joined editorial boards, a women's leadership organization board, alumni clubs, have begun adjunct teaching, and formed my own LLC. Not to mention the fact that I've had the remarkable opportunity to foray into writing through this very book! I've left countless doors open to see what the future may hold.

So how to truly answer the question of "what's next?" Well, let's just say it's complicated and in my case was nowhere near what I expected. What I learned and saw was that by being willing to fail and step outside the traditional path, an even more illuminating future surfaced. In working part-time I met lots of other women working part-time for a host of reasons. Some had private-practices, one designed jewelry on the side, and another was building an interior design company. They taught me that it was okay to have other passions outside of my field, and that, in fact, this was what gave life true meaning. It brought me back into balance. It challenged me to think about what I wanted out of life that didn't just focus on work.

In thinking about the next step, it can help to think about coloring outside of the lines. Maybe you want to teach part-time and write books. Perhaps you are going into research but also want to be involved in mentorship. Many professionals actually wind up with piecemeal careers. They teach at multiple places, or contract with different agencies. They may use their expertise to serve as a consultant. There are countless ways of doing it, and backing up to survey the lay of the land from afar can reveal new possibilities.

Your Turn!

★ *PhDilemmas: Depending upon your field, when you graduate, the economy, and pure chance, post-graduation may or may not present itself with dilemmas. Take a deep breath and assess what you need and what you have always wanted out of your life'. This is the first time in many years where you are in the driver's seat. Although it may feel like you are at the whim of human resources departments and other personnel, the power to say yes or no rests completely in your hands. Don't allow yourself to be pressured into something that doesn't feel right. Don't hesitate to try something small or part-time to get a feel for an agency or academic setting. Most importantly, try to tune in to that little voice in your head that sometimes you really don't want to listen to. It can have a lot more wisdom than we give it credit for.*

THE FIVE-YEAR PLAN

I know, it sounds strange. The five-year plan. Especially when about 5 years ago, you were writing essays documenting yours, which ended right about when your Ph.D. studies would terminate. You broadly discussed obtaining an academic career in said essay. The rest was left a bit foggy and vague so your admissions committee could selectively fill in the blanks in your favor. But think about it. What is your five-year plan now that graduate school is over? Let's say you take a one to two year post-doc. If you would like an academic route, then you're looking at an assistant professor position and getting tenure. It's pretty straightforward and laid out before you.

What happens when you don't want an academic position? What does this route look like in the industry, private, or corporate sector? Are you moving up in terms of titles, salaries, getting a directorship position? Naturally, it might take some head-scratching. The path isn't quite so obvious in non-academic careers. In fact, it might even just mean being at the position for 1-2 years until you see if you even like it. In the clinical realm, a lot of folks might decrease their patient load and increase teaching and supervision. In creative writing it might mean a position that helps you work on your novel on the side.

Maybe you want to start your own business or consulting firm one day. Perhaps your heart has always been in non-profits or work in the developing world. Or you take a position to pay the bills and work on pro-bono projects on the side until the latter becomes a sustainable part of your career. There's a possibility that international travel, exploration, and research are what interest you. I've had students passionate about archeology, African studies, and international affairs who've talked about their dream of living and studying abroad at some point in their futures. The possibilities are endless.

Depending on how much planning you care for, it may or may not be worth taking out some paper and brainstorming. Write out what the next few years looks like. But don't focus solely on work either. There might be personal goals or achievements you'd like to see realized. It can be important to leave some time for those as well. While post-docs and internships easily tell us what we might be doing for the next one to two years, it can help to have some forward thinking and envision what a five-year plan might look like.

Also, don't be shy about reading up on or even contacting professional idols. I'm always amazed when learning about the stories behind many cultural legends and how they got to where they did. That's right—I'm talking about the Diane Sawyers, Ariana Huffingtons, and Sheryl Sandbergs. Many times it was through roundabout ways, lots of persistence and passion toward making their dreams come true that they achieved such success. Seeing that even the greats struggled and stumbled, even thought about giving up on their dreams at one time or another, can be deeply comforting.

Your Turn!

★ *PhDelve: Delve into books, magazines, films, quotes, anything that inspires you. If you've ever made a vision board, then you'll know exactly what I'm talking about. If not, don't roll your eyes quite yet. Take a piece of cardboard or poster board and start flipping through newspapers, magazines, old photos, and start cutting and pasting. Pick out images that are exciting and inspiring. Words, even textures and fabrics count. I made a vision board long ago perhaps the first year of graduate school. I had photos of a yogi, a funny cartoon of a dog laying on a therapy couch, a woman feeding the hungry, and a woman hosting a Thanksgiving dinner among other images. The pictures evoked a life of balance, family, career, and happiness. Over the years, all of these images manifested in reality in one way or another. Go ahead, and make a vision board. Don't feel silly and you don't even have to show anyone. But it can help to see what inspires you and what you want more of in your life going forward. If this still doesn't strike your fancy, pick up an autobiography of a woman who you'd consider to be a success. Read up and take notes!*

WHAT IF I JUST WANT TO SETTLE DOWN?

According to one statistic, the average age of the Ph.D. graduate is 34. Yes, this is just the average. You could be significantly younger, or a bit older. What this means though is that depending on what part of the continuum you fall upon, other needs may start to take precedence. Perhaps you already have children and want to back off from work pursuits to focus on them. As I've discussed before, you may be in the mental space of wanting to establish that relationship in the first place to be able to get married and choose whether or not to have children.

What many women encounter in these decisions is a sense of guilt and fears of having disappointed advisors, colleagues, and perhaps even themselves. They wonder if it's acceptable to have spent so much time on a Ph.D. only to put it aside and pursue other ambitions. In my program, one of my friends and colleagues found love early on in graduate school and was married. One of the young junior faculty approached her and shared that she would advise against having children while in graduate school. The faculty member had children of her own, a busy life, and countless other personal factors impacting her viewpoint. It is likely that she truly did have the best intentions at heart when sharing this with my friend. But it also can't be denied that hearing such a message post marital bliss can feel like a slap in the face.

The lack of female faculty in the first place, those with young children, or even stable marriages can be tough to find in some departments. I recall being amazed when meeting graduate students at other schools where they had female mentors who were strong role models of what it meant to be a professional, wife, and mother. These mentors taught their mentees the value of placing boundaries and showed that women most definitely had a place in academia that wasn't shoved in some hidden corner somewhere. They were fully productive, achieved tenure, and appeared to have well-balanced happy families.

This said, if you want to have children, settle down, move back closer to family, it is your prerogative. No one in the academy has any say over that. I watched with a combination of awe and admiration as graduate student women in my department defended Master's theses, became pregnant, gave birth, took a leave, came back, did their dissertation and so on. Naturally, it took a bit longer to complete all their requirements, but they often seemed to have a contentment about them. No matter what professors or advisors thought about them or their program of research, they were involved in something far bigger and more important. They had little ones, partners, and a community that extended far beyond the reaches of the academy.

Do what feels right to you. If you want to take a break and pursue motherhood or date seriously for the first time, go for it. The reality we sometimes feel compelled to tiptoe around is that of women's biological clocks. As science has made significant advances and more is being understood about women's fertility, the picture has changed somewhat. Still, the human body has limits and, for many women, there is somewhat of a finite conception window before fertility clinics and treatments become the next option for those who are not yet open to or ready for adoption.

Your Turn!

★ *PhDecisions: It's all up to you now! Maybe you are ready to put that degree to work, pronto. On the other hand, you might just need a* break, some time to relax and figure out what is really needed. There is the likelihood you can balance finding a professional position and getting married or having children, or just taking care of the ones you have! Whatever your fancy, the decision rests within. Certainly, if you are partnered, they will have some influence and say as well. But if not, it can help to assess once more what your overarching plans were all along. Remember that once you receive your Ph.D. you can put it to use whenever you want. There are no expiration dates! Though some will try to warn you about being off the job market and difficulties getting back in, that only leads to an endless cycle of being overworked and burnt out. With this degree you can go no higher in your field and it opens up many doors. Don't feel rushed or pressured into using it ASAP. Your life, well-being, and happiness are really what are most important.

THE PHDIVA'S CREED

Throughout this book, I have aimed to elucidate, educate, and inspire to the best of my abilities. By no means may what I have shared painted a complete picture of what any one woman's journey up the ivory tower may look like. There may have been parts of my story that resonated and others that seemed completely off base. But in my training as a psychologist and multicultural researcher, I have a strong belief in empowering the next generation of scholars. Part of this work is through the process of sharing our own narratives. As a woman, I believe in placing before other women a platinum pedestal upon which to level out the playing field for them in times when they may be discounted, ignored, or treated unfairly due to their gender or any other demographic factor.

I've aimed to be true to my story and also the story of the countless graduate student women I have seen in my therapy office as well as students I have mentored and taught. I've also adopted my own version of feminism that may or may not jibe with our traditional or modern feminist scholars. Naturally, my view is shaped by having been brought up in an immigrant family, having lived in both highly conservative and liberal areas. It is also influenced by a desire to integrate pieces of all philosophies to create a holistic understanding of what is means to be a female scholar. Below, is my final hope and wish for not only all my readers, but women in academia at large.

I, _____, Ph.D., PhDiva, vow:
(insert name here)

- to support my fellow woman and man kind with kindness, character, integrity, and grace.
- to always be inquisitive, test the boundaries in my field but also in my life.
- to approach difficult situations with dignity and tact.
- to not apologize for the unique expression of my gender.
- to hold my head up high and not allow negative professional criticism to become internalized.
- to never feel like an imposter.
- to take care of myself fully in every sense of the word.
- to learn to relax, laugh, and be a model of self-care for other female professionals in my field.
- to learn to listen to my own intuition and not apologize for the answers that may come from a place you cannot always see or understand.
- to be brave enough to stand up for what may sometimes be unpopular or stigmatized.
- to welcome fellow women into the field, provide mentorship, support, and allow them to feel included.
- to acknowledge the privilege I've been given to pursue higher education and work to empower those who may need my assistance.

- to fully and deeply experience the process from beginning to end, daring, dreaming, and dancing in the department as all PhDivas deserve.

Your Turn!

★ *PhDiva: It's a wrap! Read the creed, add to it, or write your own. Tear it out from Appendix D if you'd like and post it in a prominent place where you can see it and be reminded of this invaluable achievement you've attained. Remind yourself of all the points regularly, perhaps highlighting the ones you need to remember the most. Or if you are anything like me, a little bit of glitter pen underlining never hurt anyone. Go ahead, be a diva about it!*

APPENDIX A

Draft Academic Plan

Freshman Year

Fall	Winter	Spring

Sophomore Year

Fall	Winter	Spring

Junior Year

Fall	Winter	Spring

Senior Year

Fall	Winter	Spring

APPENDIX B

E.M.P.O.W.E.R. Checklist

	Monday	Tuesday	Wednesday	Thursday	Friday	Saturday	Sunday
Exercise run 3x/wk	✗		✗		✗		
Meditation daily 15 min	✗	✗	✗			✗	✗
Positivity inspirational reading			✗				✗
Outdoors biking 4x/wk		✗	✗	✗			✗
Work learn guitar						✗	
Enlighten Big Brothers Club volunteer							✗
Relationships coffee with friends 2x/wk	✗					✗	
Mood (1-10 Best)	7	8	9	5	6	9	8

	Monday	Tuesday	Wednesday	Thursday	Friday	Saturday	Sunday
Exercise _____							
Meditation _____							
Positivity _____							
Outdoors _____							
Work _____							
Enlighten _____							
Relationships _____							
Mood (1-10 Best)							

APPENDIX C
Self-Care Apps

1) Health/Nutrition Apps
   Water Your Body Lite (Daniel Floyd)
   Lumen Trails Daily Organizer (Lumen Spark LLC)
   Pacer-Pedometer Plus Weight and BMI Management (Michael Caldwell)
   Runtastic Pedometer Step Counter (runtastic)
   Calorie Counter and Diet Tracker (MyFitnessPal.com)
2) Sleep Apps
   Sleep Stream 2 (Explosive Apps)
   Smart Alarm Clock (Plus Sports)
   Relaxing Sounds (Sonotap)
   Sleep Cycle (Maciek Drejak labs)- this one is not free but
      is very much worth the investment!
3) Mood Tracking Apps
   MyMoodTracker Lite (Aspyre Solutions)
   Moody Me (MedHelp)
   Stigma Journal Daily Gratitude Diary (Daniel Seider)
   Optimism (Optimism Apps)
4) Gratitude Apps
   Thankful (Eddy Street Productions, LLC)
   Happy Feed (Matthew Kandler)
   Gratitude Journal 365 (Benjamin Hsu)
   Happiness Wizard (Success Wizard, Inc.)
5) Meditation Apps
   Headspace.com (Headspace Meditation Limited)
   Take a Break! (Meditation Oasis)
   Buddhist Meditation Lite (Jun Li)
   Lotus Bud Mindfulness Bell (Chad Sager)
   re-mindful (Random APPS of Kindness)

APPENDIX D

The PhDiva's Creed

I, _____, Ph.D., PhDiva, vow:
(insert name here)

TO support my fellow woman and man kind with kindness, character, integrity, and grace.

TO always be inquisitive, test the boundaries in my field but also in my life.

TO approach difficult situations with dignity and tact.

TO not apologize for the unique expression of my gender.

TO hold my head up high and not allow negative professional criticism to become internalized.

TO never feel like an imposter.

TO take care of myself fully in every sense of the word.

TO learn to relax, laugh, and be a model of self-care for other female professionals in my field.

TO learn to listen to my own intuition and not apologize for the answers that may come from a place you cannot always see or understand.

TO be brave enough to stand up for what may sometimes be unpopular or stigmatized.

TO welcome fellow women into the field, provide mentorship, support, and allow them to feel included.

TO acknowledge the privilege I've been given to pursue higher education and work to empower those who may need my assistance.

TO fully and deeply experience the process from beginning to end, daring, dreaming, and dancing in the department as all PhDivas deserve.

TO _____

TO _____

X _____
Signature